FEMINISM AND PSYCHOANALYSIS

LANGUAGE, DISCOURSE, SOCIETY
Editors: Stephen Heath and Colin MacCabe

Published
VISION AND PAINTING: The Logic of the Gaze
Norman Bryson
FEMINISM AND PSYCHOANALYSIS: The Daughter's Seduction
Jane Gallop
ON LAW AND IDEOLOGY
Paul Hirst
JAMES JOYCE AND THE REVOLUTION OF THE WORD
Colin MacCabe
THE TALKING CURE: Essays in Psychoanalysis and Language
Colin MacCabe (*editor*)
PSYCHOANALYSIS AND CINEMA: The Imaginary Signifier
Christian Metz
LANGUAGE, SEMANTICS AND IDEOLOGY
Michel Pécheux
THE MAKING OF THE READER: Language and Subjectivity in Modern American,
English and Irish Poetry
David Trotter

Forthcoming
STATE OF NATURE: Ethnography and Origins
Beverley Brown and Judith Ennew
TO REPRESENT WOMAN? The Representation of Sexual Differences in the Visual
Media
Elizabeth Cowie
CONDITIONS OF MUSIC
Alan Durant
THE MEANINGS OF LANGUAGE
Alan Durant, Colin MacCabe and Paul Abbott (*editors*)
UNDERSTANDING BECKETT
Peter Gidal
THREE ESSAYS ON SUBJECTIVITY
Stephen Heath
THE GENEALOGY OF MORAL FORMS: Foucault, Nietzsche, Donzelot
Jeffrey Minson
POUND'S NOMANCLATTER: Language, Sexuality and Ideology in the 'Cantos'
Jean-Michel Rabaté
THE CASE OF PETER PAN OR THE IMPOSSIBILITY OF CHILDREN'S FICTION
Jacqueline Rose
FEMINISMS A CONCEPTURE HISTORY
Denise Riley

FEMINISM AND PSYCHOANALYSIS
The Daughter's Seduction

Jane Gallop

MACMILLAN

First published 1982
Reprinted 1982, 1983, 1986, 1990

Published by
MACMILLAN ACADEMIC AND PROFESSIONAL LTD
Houndmills, Basingstoke, Hampshire RG21 2XS
and London
Companies and representatives
throughout the world

Printed in Hong Kong

ISBN 0–333–29471–8 (hardcover)
ISBN 0–333–29472–6 (paperback)

For Peggy Kamuf

Contents

Contents

Contents

Acknowledgements

I would like to thank Miami University and the Center for Twentieth Century Studies, University of Wisconsin–Milwaukee, for financial support for this book.

I would like to thank the following people for reading versions of chapters and offering valuable suggestions for revision: Richard Blau, Tom Conley, James Creech, Jesse Dickson, Britton Harwood, Stephen Heath, Neil Hertz, Peggy Kamuf and Naomi Schor.

Chapters 1, 3 and 6 are revised versions of articles originally published in, respectively, *Diacritics*, vol. 5, no. 4, *Diacritics*, vol. 6, no. 4 and *Sub-Stance*, no. 26.

Introduction

Feminism and Psychoanalysis: The Daughter's Seduction studies the relation between contemporary feminist theory and the psychoanalysis of Jacques Lacan. Through readings of the signal texts which stand at the intersection of French psychoanalysis and feminism, it enters into a network of problems: problems of sexual difference, of desire, of reading, of writing, of power, of family, of phallocentrism and of language. Thus, while working to produce an acquaintance with psychoanalytic and feminist thinking current in France, it is continually posing questions that are not specific to the exotic space of France, but which are equally nagging at any Anglophone site of this text: the sites of its writing as well as of the reading of it.

Although I have taken a constant care not to mystify the uninitiated by esoteric reference or jargon, this book is not intended to be simply an introduction to or a translation of an existent body of knowledge but rather a contribution to the sort of thinking it describes–that is, a contribution to French psychoanalytic feminist thought from the vantage-point of these English-speaking shores. Both French feminism and French psychoanalysis are fields of stubborn polemic between various exclusive little circles. The advantage of writing from here is the possibility of creating exchanges between the discourses of people who do not speak to each other.

In this book, the writer's viewpoint, the narrative voice, changes–from chapter to chapter, even within chapters. I consider this to be one of its strengths. In this context, strength is defined not in the polemic sense of ability to stand one's ground, but in the psychoanalytic sense of capacity for change, flexibility, ability to learn, to be touched and moved by contact with others.

The repeated gesture of the book is to set up what appears to be an opposition between two thinkers or terms, and then to move beyond the belligerence of opposition to an exchange between the terms. The most stubborn opposition is the continual constitution of 'opposite sexes' which blocks the possibility of a relation between them. Another inevitable opposition in this network is that between psychoanalysis and feminism or, in other words, between psychoanalysis and politics. In all these cases the goal and the method of this book is to alter that relation from unyielding opposition into a contact between their specific differences–a contact that might yield some real change.

In its basic project, this book is the continual working of a dialectical tension between 'psychoanalysis' and 'feminism'. The book claims to *be* psychoanalytic and feminist. Yet I am not a psychoanalyst and others have questioned my right to the label 'feminist'. I would not endorse most of the traditional practices of either psychoanalysis or feminism, but hope that the encounter of the two can bring each to its most radical potential. Psychoanalysis, for instance, can unsettle feminism's tendency to accept a traditional, unified, rational, puritanical self–a self supposedly free from the violence of desire. In its turn, feminism can shake up psychoanalysis's tendency to think itself apolitical but in fact be conservative by encouraging people to adapt to an unjust social structure.

I do not consider this need of each for the other as a sign of some weakness. Rather that in order to exercise the strength of flexibility they must encounter each other, for in mutual exclusion they are liable to seek the strength of rigid defence. The radical potential in their marriage is not a mystical fusion obliterating all difference and conflict, but a provocative contact which opens each to what is not encompassed by the limits of its identity.

The question of identity poses itself in various fashions throughout. Both psychoanalysis and feminism can be seen as efforts to call into question a rigid identity that cramps and binds. But both also tend to want to produce a 'new identity', one that will now be adequate and authentic. I hold the Lacanian view that any identity will necessarily be alien and constraining. I do not believe in some 'new identity' which would be adequate and authentic. But I do not seek some sort of liberation from identity. That would lead only to another form of paralysis–the oceanic passivity of undifferentiation. Identity must be continually assumed and immediately called into question.

In a manner analogous to the dialogue between psychoanalysis and feminism, each chapter of the book stages the encounter between texts of at least two authors. This method is a way of getting more out of the texts read, something that goes beyond the boundaries which an author might want to impose upon his or her work. The notions of integrity and closure in a text are like that of virginity in a body. They assume that if one does not respect the boundaries between inside and outside, one is 'breaking and entering', violating a property. As long as the fallacies of integrity and closure are upheld, a desire to penetrate becomes a desire for rape. I hope to engage in some intercourse with these textual bodies that has a different economy, one in which entry and interpenetration do not mean disrespect or violation because they are not based upon the myth of the book's or the self's or the body's virginal wholeness. But rather upon the belief that, if words there be or body there be, somewhere there is a desire for dialogue, intercourse, exchange.

Juliet Mitchell's *Psychoanalysis and Feminism*—echoed in my title—is the point of departure for our journey into French thought. Mitchell's effort pointed in the direction of Lacan, but did not finally depart from familiar Anglophone feminist grounds. I read Mitchell's book with a cognizance of the problems faced by a more thorough consideration of Lacanian theory.

In the second chapter Lacan meets Ernest Jones over the question of phallocentrism. Jones was one of the first to decry the phallocentrism of psychoanalytic theory, whereas Lacan declares the phallus 'the privileged signifier'. But feminism does not necessarily find its ally in the man who theorizes the relation between the sexes according to how, in all fairness, it ought to be.

Lacan is with a number of women in the third chapter, which is a reading of Lacan's twentieth seminar (on the question of 'What does Woman want?') along with issue 58 of the French intellectual review *L'Arc*, devoted to Lacan and written by women. The question of Lacan's relation to feminism is posed more pointedly in this chapter. This is the first moment when feminist criticism of and resistance to Lacan is represented.

The third chapter also introduces Luce Irigaray who plays the female lead, opposite Lacan, in this book. In Chapter 2, Michèle Montrelay is introduced to liven up the dialogue between Lacan and Jones. Although there is no chapter specifically devoted to a reading of Montrelay, she appears in three chapters, since her presentation of a Lacanian view of female sexuality has been crucial for my understanding of it.

The fourth chapter returns to Lacan's twentieth seminar, this time reading it to the accompaniment of Stephen Heath's feminist critique. This meeting of two men around the Woman Question opens up issues of men's relation to feminism. A British reading of Lacan also reimposes notions of the gap between Anglo-American and French feminism. Across this gap jumps the spark of desire that ignites *Feminism and Psychoanalysis*.

The middle chapter of the book reads Irigaray with Freud on the relation between the daughter and the father. This is perhaps the central question in the book, a centrality reflected in the similarity between the book's subtitle and the title of this long, central chapter–'The Father's Seduction'. The roles of father and daughter are given to Lacan and Irigaray as well as to Psychoanalysis and Feminism. But because this father–daughter relation is a seduction, the roles become more complicated, more equivocal, more yielding.

The sixth chapter represents the struggle between Irigaray and Lacan. I introduce the Marquis de Sade into that meeting to play the truth-liberating role of the jester. Passing through Sade, who makes the incestuous seduction explicit, allows the book to move beyond its repeated confrontations and homages to Father Lacan.

Irigaray, in the next chapter, meets Eugénie Lemoine-Luccioni, a woman analyst who has remained loyal to Lacan. The encounter between these two women leads us to a crucial subject, the conflict between psychoanalysis and politics, and also poses some questions about the relation between the phallus and the penis. It ends by introducing the problem of motherhood.

The eighth chapter takes up the question of the mother in a reading of Julia Kristeva with Irigaray. Although throughout the book Irigaray has had the heroic role of the daughter, this position is now criticized in relation not to the father but to the mother. Here, Kristeva's assumption of the role of the mother presents a possible way through the daughter's dilemma.

The final chapter is a reading of Hélène Cixous's and Catherine Clément's book *La jeune née* along with Freud's Dora and Cixous's Dora. This unsettling encounter is already present in Clément's and Cixous's book, a book which is the very sort of dialogue which my book tries to stage. Neither Lacan nor Irigaray appear in this final chapter, which moves beyond the closed circle of the family in an attempt to prod psychoanalysis out of its comfortable domain and into a more radical forum.

The book begins by calling into question certain feminist assumptions through the agency of Lacanian psychoanalysis. Its ends by calling into question certain psychoanalytic positions through the agency of feminist writing. The seduction that has taken place has been rather complex. Feminism (the daughter) has been seduced out of her resistance to psychoanalysis (the father). The father has been seduced out of his impassive self-mastery and into showing his desire. But the seduction has, I hope, moved both out of the familial roles of father and daughter so that they will no longer be locked into their vicious circle. Perhaps the seduction of both is the introduction of heterogeneity (sexuality, violence, economic class conflict) into the closed circle of the family.

Psychoanalysis often considers revolutionary conflict along the parent–child model, thus reassimilating larger social issues into the familial domain. But feminism, too, often falls for a familial interpretation of power relations. For instance, when it complains about men in power, it endows them with the sort of unified, phallic sovereignty that characterizes an absolute monarch, and which little resembles actual power in our social, economic structures. This monarchic model of power reproduces the daughter's view of the father. Perhaps *The Daughter's Seduction*, the encounter between psychoanalysis and feminism, by dephallicizing the father, can avoid the pitfall of familial thinking in order to have greater effect upon the much more complex power relations that structure our world.

1 Psychoanalysis and Feminism

Juliet Mitchell's *Psychoanalysis and Feminism*[1] would seem to insert itself in a broad tradition of books in whose titles one finds 'and' tucked snugly between two powerful nouns. In such cases, the conjunction serves to indicate either the author's study of little- or well-known intersections between the two domains, or a projection of a possible, fruitful union. Within this tradition the most strenuous task allotted to 'and' might be to connect two substantives that are totally indifferent to each other. Yet, this is not the fate of Mitchell's 'and', which lies serenely on the cover in denial of the battle that is raging between psychoanalysis and feminism. This 'and' bridges the gap between two combatants; it runs back and forth holding its white flag as high as possible. Although, of the two, feminism has shown itself to be the most belligerent, psychoanalysis has not been known to come begging for forgiveness or reconciliation. The quiescent tradition of 'and' as mainstay for peaceful coexistence is belied by the assertiveness of Mitchell's step.

Her boldness stands in fullest relief in America, where feminists' views of Freud run the gamut from considering him an evil man, and one of women's greatest enemies, to seeing him as a brilliant dreamer, who was either blind to the conditions around him or did not look beyond those conditions. Following both the developments of psychoanalysis and the course of feminism peculiar to different countries, she sets up a 'descending scale of opposition by feminists to Freud' (p. 297) and finds the greatest opposition in America, most interest on the continent, with England in between. So it seems fitting that Mitchell, one of England's best-known feminists, should take on the project of importing the continental feminist interest in Freud, in an effort to combat the American opposition to psychoanalysis. Although, at one point, she mentions Scandinavian feminists (p. 297), she is, in fact,

1

leaning not upon a general continental but upon a specifically
French feminism, and especially upon the group 'Psychoanalysis
and Politics', towards which the introduction of the book points
for general orientation. Having based her undertaking upon a
certain French feminism (and, as we shall see later, upon a certain French reading of Freud), Mitchell speaks up within the
generally anti-Freudian atmosphere of English-speaking feminism, not as Shulamith Firestone did for a partial, piecemeal ac-
ceptance, but for a serious reading of Freud, one which does not
evade his unpleasant analysis of the feminine position, penis-envy
and all.

Mitchell's book offers a harsh critique of a pervasive blindness
in American feminism to Freud's analyses, a blindness founded
upon a distaste for the situations he describes. Mitchell is at her
sharpest when analyzing the distortions inflicted by feminists
upon Freud's text and his discoveries. She ties the feminists' distortions to the work of Wilhelm Reich and R. D. Laing, whom
she sees as having strongly influenced the radical ideology of the
sixties that gave birth to modern feminism. These critiques give
the book a path-clearing thrust which makes it essential reading
for anyone interested in feminist ideology. Mitchell is not just
saying something else about Freud; she is saying that what all the
other feminists before have said is wrong. And Mitchell is saying
that their errors have very serious consequences for the feminist
analysis of woman's psychology and woman's situation: in short,
grave consequences for feminism's effectiveness.

For Mitchell, the feminist misunderstanding of Freud is not a
simple chance happening. She aptly shows her readers certain
traits shared by all the feminist distortions: above all, an implicit
denial of Freud's unconscious and of his concept of a sexuality
that is not inscribed within the bounds of actual interpersonal
relations. Although feminists before have differed in their stand
on Freud, Mitchell's contribution lies in tying their various positions together, in seeing in them a structure and not merely
diverse contingencies. 'Each of these authors, after paying tribute
to the discovery of the importance of sexuality in human life, proceeds to deny it by converting it, after all, into something as
generalized as "life-energy"—a generality from which Freud
originally rescued it and to which, time and again, he had to
forbid it to return' (p. 352). The 'time and again' points toward
some tendency inherent in the Freudian discovery to revert to

pre-Freudian concepts. Mitchell delineates the work of such a tendency by describing the odyssey of Freud's discovery through diverse misunderstandings. She carefully pinpoints that which she considers most original, most 'Freudian' in Freud's work; then she shows how the post-Freudian has been but a repeated return to the pre-Freudian. The possibility of this return is structured into the difficulty, the audacity of Freud's discovery. Even Freud was not immune to it: 'Freud was as capable as anyone else of being pre-Freudian—but he had less to gain from it' (p. 323). Obviously, 'pre-Freudian' cannot here be an expression of temporal relationship as usually understood. And if not all of Freud is 'Freudian', it is essential that we understand what Mitchell is referring to. The 'Freudian' Freud placed a premium on 'psychical reality' over actual 'reality'. Freud's contribution to man's understanding of himself is a description of the human being in culture, not of the natural animal, man. Distortion of Freud always seems to go in the direction of some sort of biologism. Hence his descriptions of man's inscription in culture are interpreted as prescriptions for normality based on nature.

One of the first to fall back into biologism, in an attempt to go beyond Freud, specifically on the question of women, was Karen Horney, who has gained a readership among modern feminists looking for a theorist of woman's psychology. Naturally, women's liberation has chosen Horney over Freud: she decries the unfairness of woman's lot while he, according to feminists, fails to do so. Mitchell's criticism of Horney suggests that the latter's seeming radicalism is actually quite reactionary. 'The male analyst, [Horney] claims, theorizes about women much as the little boy speculates about the little girl, and women submit to being this receptacle of masculine phantasy—often against their true nature. Worthy as were Horney's intentions, . . . nothing could have been more disastrous for the future of the psychoanalysis of women than this call to a "true nature"' (p. 128).

In a movement similar to her perceptive reading of Horney, Mitchell's criticism of other theorists influential in provoking modern American feminists' opposition to Freud repeatedly underlines these same points: a misreading of description as prescription and a valorization of 'reality' over psychic life. It seems that at the heart of every reaction against Freud is some sort of essentialism. Freud subverted the traditional belief that alienation was secondary, that it acted upon some essential, unified

ego, thus perverting it, and alienating it from itself. Mitchell
analyzes how all the writers discussed in the book return, either
explicitly or implicitly, to a belief in an essential self, just as she
finds Horney basing her psychoanalysis of women upon a 'true
nature' that has submitted itself to distortion. The unwillingness
to see that the Freudian discovery points to a self that, unlike
Laing's 'divided self', is primordially alienated is the refusal of the
unconscious, the Freudian unconscious.

As Mitchell says, 'The Freud the feminists have inherited is a
long way off-centre' (p. 301). The Freud Mitchell wants to bring
to the feminists is not the one who, unfortunately, might have
said 'anatomy is destiny', but a Freud who analyzed and described
how man, primordially alienated, 'makes' himself in culture. She
is advocating a Freud virtually unknown to American feminists,
who associate Freud with normalizing adaptation to the *status
quo*. In fact, the Freud Mitchell supports did not believe in
adaptation; and so she hopes that by introducing this Freud, the
'Freudian' Freud, she can supplement a serious lack in modern
Anglo-American feminism. Thus one of the meanings the 'and' of
the book's title must maintain is that of an addition: Mitchell
would add psychoanalysis to feminism to make feminism stronger,
richer, wiser, better.

In her Introduction Mitchell states, 'If advocacy of Freud is the
theme of this book, the conversation is at all times with the many
aspects of feminism' (p. xix). In a book where the author writes of
the constitution of the ego in alienation, where in a footnote she
writes, 'Freud had his analyst in Fliess, the recipient and, in a
sense, originator, of Freud's letters' (p. 62n), the role of the interlocutor cannot be taken lightly. In her specific readings of the
feminists, where she is at her most incisive, Mitchell is nastiest,
wittiest and most playful in her language. These chapters are
characterized by a stinging informality which offers a sharp contrast to both the critical respect evident in her chapters on Reich
and Laing and the objective exposition of the earliest chapters,
the chapters on Freud. Later, after the section on the feminists,
she becomes more serious, more difficult, until she reaches the
heartfelt projects of the last chapter, the chapter entitled 'The
Cultural Revolution'.

Besides her major thesis that all the feminist writers are
denying the nonbiologism of Freud's discovery, Mitchell argues

that much of their criticism consists of trivial complaints against Freud the man. In the earlier chapters which set forth Freud's theories she quickly dismisses the 'red herring' that is the examination of Freud's life (p. 107). Yet, interestingly, the repudiation of this trivial *ad hominem* argument returns continually. In a curious footnote Mitchell writes: 'If in this account I have defended Freud's character as well as his theory of psychoanalysis, it is not because I consider it in any way important.... But the subject matter of psychoanalysis makes Freud particularly vulnerable to this critical red herring. My "defence" should thus be seen as an irrelevance, introduced to counter an irrelevance—not a very defensible aim!' (p. 332n). 'An irrelevance introduced to counter an irrelevance' seems to underline the odd complicity between the partners of a conversation, Mitchell's 'conversation...with the many aspects of feminism'. In the light of her declaration that interest in Freud's character is a 'critical red herring', it is significant that *Psychoanalysis and Feminism* includes a seventeen-page appendix called 'Psychoanalysis and Vienna at the Turn of the Century', the largest part of which contains examples of how Freud, for his time, was often quite liberal with regard to women. Why does Mitchell devote so much space to 'an irrelevance introduced to counter an irrelevance'?

It seems that the fanciful prose in Mitchell's reading of the feminist texts and her repeated discussion of the *ad hominem* argument are indicators of a continuing wish to distance herself from these feminists, to position herself apart from them, a wish that must remain unfulfilled because it is impossible to keep her stated project—'a conversation...with the many aspects of feminism'—constantly separate from a conversation with actual feminists. She is locked into an exchange with those whom she is trying to transcend. Hence she is most forcefully lucid in criticizing these her interlocutors, and weakest in synthesizing a version of Freud that goes outside the limits of that conversation. While undertaking to introduce psychoanalysis into the bounds of a certain English-speaking feminism, she excises that which does not fit within those bounds, rather than question the limits themselves.

Mitchell's argument touches upon recent psychoanalytic developments in France, especially the work of Jacques Lacan, which is virtually unknown to American feminists. Lacan has been a powerful influence upon French feminist thought. Much of Mitchell's project follows Lacan's direction in its emphasis on fidelity to the originality of Freud's text and in its denial of Freud's biologism. Yet, oddly, her relation to Lacan's theory is never made explicit. For a reader acquainted with Lacan, he functions as a very present absence, an absence inadequately exorcised by Mitchell's reference to him.

In the long and rather confusing chapter 'The Different Self, the Phallus and the Father', which contains Mitchell's most radical statements in the register of psychoanalysis (quite different from her most radical feminist statements), Lacan is mentioned frequently and his works are quoted several times. Yet Mitchell provides no continuity between the specific points of Lacanian theory; she includes in this chapter no sign as to whether the material between these points is in agreement with his theory, derived from his theory, in opposition to it, or simply indifferent. Apart from affording the reader no clear conception of what Lacan is actually about, the chapter is hard to follow. Above all, the reader remains unsure of the relationship between feminism and this discussion of a primordially alienated self, a dead father, and a symbolic phallus. And, continuing into the next (and last) section of Mitchell's book, one finds that the most difficult points in 'The Different Self...' have been left behind: they are never integrated into her general theory.

In this chapter, Mitchell has recourse to a discussion of the difference between desire and need—one of Lacan's references in his distinction of the instinctual from the condition of man in culture, a distinction Mitchell wishes to uphold. According to Mitchell, 'The baby *needs* food, protection, etc.; his mother then *demands* certain responses from him, as for instance in toilet training; in learning to understand the nature of his mother's demand, the child comes to desire to satisfy her desire. Desire is therefore always a question of a significant interrelationship, desire is always the desire of the other' (p. 396). On the same page Mitchell goes on to explain that in the absence of the breast or whatever is needed, 'need changes to demand (articulation), and if unsatisfied or unreciprocated, to desire'. There seems to be a contradiction between these two quotations: in the first, the baby's need changes to desire through the workings of the mother's demand; in the second passage the need itself changes to 'demand (articulation)' and then, through the cruelty of the outside world, to desire. Neither of these follows the Lacanian conception of the relationship between 'need', 'the demand' and 'desire'. Of course, Mitchell is not obliged to present the Lacanian conception; however, 'need', 'the demand', and 'desire' are articulated with each other in Lacan's works in a formulation that resembles the two quoted above, yet is essentially different. Lacan relies upon no contingency to link these concepts. In Mitchell's first formulation the mother could feed the child without demanding toilet training. In the second, an 'if' appears: 'if unsatisfied or unreciprocated' implies the possibility of 'if satisfied or reciprocated'. Yet this un-Lacanian explanation is sandwiched between two direct references to Lacan upon whom Mitchell is leaning in order to define the phallus.

Here then is this very relation as it appears at one point in Lacan's work: 'Let us at this point examine the effects of this presence [of signifier]. There is first of all a deviation of man's needs due to the fact that he speaks, in that in so far as his needs are subjugated to the demand they come back to him alienated. This is not the effect of his real dependency. . . but of the putting into signifying/significant form as such and of the fact that it is from the locus of the Other that his message is emitted. That which thus finds itself alienated in needs constitutes an *Urverdrängung* [primal repression], by being unable, by hypothesis, to articulate itself in the demand, but which appears in an offshoot, is what presents itself in man as desire.'[2] By placing the emphasis on 'this is not the effect of his real dependency', which is directed to just such contingent explanations as those of Mitchell cited above, Lacan, unlike Mitchell, grounds his argument entirely in the effect of the signifier, that is, the effect of language. And curiously, there is a hint of this linguistic structuring in Mitchell's wording 'demand (articulation)' and maybe even in 'significant interrelationship', although 'significant' does not have the same direct relationship to the signifier as does the French 'signifiant', translated above as 'signifying/significant'.

If Mitchell is trying to paraphrase Lacan's exposition, she is taking a needlessly treacherous path. By not including language explicitly in her elucidation of Lacan's theory she arrives at formulations based upon contingencies. On the next page (the conclusion of this chapter) she apologizes for her omission of the discussion of language in the following manner:

The situation is infinitely more complicated than this reduced and condensed version, above all because I have left out. . . what really amounts to the *whole framework and thrust of the theory*: the importance of language. In a sense this is an *inex-*

cusable distortion of a theory but one necessitated by the specific concern: the psychology of women under patriarchy. The absence of any reference to language—the very world into which the human child is born and by which he is named and placed (man does not speak, language 'speaks' him) *can only be excused by the inexhaustible number of other omissions*, all of which, in that they refer to the way mankind becomes human and lives his humanity, have bearing on the formation and meaning of feminine psychology. (pp. 397–8, my italics)

What is most unsettling about this generally disconcerting passage are two closely related contradictions: first, that 'an inexcusable distortion of a theory' could in any way 'be excused' (and that, like the 'irrelevance introduced to counter an irrelevance', the distorting omission is 'excused' by 'other omissions'); second, that what is stressed as 'the whole framework and thrust of the theory' should be on a par with an 'inexhaustible number of other omissions'.

Language, it seems, is fated to share with Lacan the position of ghost (the dead Father) in *Psychoanalysis and Feminism*. Yet, although language's relegation to the margins is no more easily explained than Lacan's, this second omission can perhaps illuminate the first. For, whether Mitchell is referring to Lacan here or not, 'the theory' whose 'whole framework and thrust' is 'the importance of language' *is* Lacan's theory. His interpretation of Freud consists of reading the letter of Freud's text in the light of his own distillation of modern (structural) linguistics. Lacan's theory cannot be presented coherently without a major discussion of the function of language. Hence the 'present absence' of Lacan discussed above is already an omission of 'the importance of language'. Perhaps this, too, stems from Mitchell's having trapped herself into a conversation, not with feminism, but with specific feminists—feminists who reflect the way American psychoanalysis ignores the ego-subverting significance of language.

Certainly a theory of language is not, and should not be, outside the bounds of feminist analysis. If we believe, as Mitchell does, that it is crucial that a lucid feminism throw off the influence of a biologistic, normalizing reading of Freud, then it is necessary to see 'civilization's discontents' as structurally inscribed into civilization and, thus, to ward off the reformisms of contingency-based explanations. Mitchell begins on that path, but her confusion in the chapter on 'The Different Self . . .' indicates that her formulations are inadequate for avoiding contingent explanations. An inclusion of language, especially Lacan's brand of structural linguistics, might have evaded some of those pitfalls of domestication. Without it, Mitchell–locked into her dialogue with those whose 'empiricism run riot denies more than the unconscious; it denies any attribute of the mind other than rationality' (p. 354)–falls back into that kind of common sense which underlies her interlocutors' belief in a rational, utility-based explanation for human behaviour.

TREE

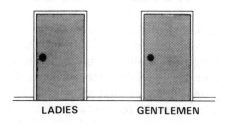

LADIES   GENTLEMEN

FIGURE 1

'The Insistence of the Letter in the Unconscious'[3] is one of the major essays in which Lacan exposes his theory of the signifier. It is in this essay, at a moment important for its presentation of the inextricable relation between the influence of language and sexual differentiation, that Lacan introduces the drawings in Figure 1.

The first image is an example of the classic method of presenting the relation between the signifier and the signified: a one-to-one correspondence between the word and the 'thing'. The 'meaning' of the word 'tree' can be learned through the drawing of the thing 'tree' which illustrates it: the word 'stands for' the thing. This classic manner of understanding the relationship between signifier and signified is totally inadequate. Lacan produces the second image to underline that inadequacy. Here the relationship between the words and the doors they indicate is stunningly more complex than any one-to-one correlation that might be assumed to operate in the first drawing. Since they refer to two identical doors, the pair of signifiers in the second illustration can only be understood (1) in relation to each other (each is 'not the other'), and (2) in what Lacan calls a 'signifying chain' (by the contexts in which these signifiers have been learned).

Lacan then relates the following story which uses the second image as its illustration. 'A train arrives at a station. A little boy and a little girl, brother and sister, are seated in a compartment face to face next to the window through which the buildings along the station platform can be seen passing as the train pulls to a stop. "Look," says the brother, "we're at Ladies!" "Idiot," replies his sister, "can't you see we're at Gentlemen?"'[4] In this story each child is able to see only one of the rest rooms; thus, each one sees an image which is more like the first drawing than the second. The first drawing leads one to be confident that words have delimitable 'things' which they 'mean'. Interestingly, it is the girl who sees 'Gentlemen' and the boy who sees 'Ladies'; as if one could only see the sex one is not, as if only the sex one is outside of could be perceived as a whole, unified locus. The 'psychical consequences of the anatomical distinction between the sexes' have a structure similar to that of the situation in this anecdote. Through the biological given of sitting on one side of the compartment or the other, each sex is placed in a structure, and as such is unable to see that structure. The biological differences are only of import to men and women in so far as they institute the subject into the play of the signifier, a play unknown as long as one accepts the first model of language, the model of one-to-one correspondence.

Yet, whether the subject knows it or not, he must function in relation to an arbitrary and thus absolute boundary between the two realms of Ladies and Gentlemen, a boundary installed irrevocably upon his horizon through the advent of the signifier. 'Ladies and Gentlemen will be henceforth for these children two countries towards which each of their souls will strive on divergent wings, and between which a cessation of hostilities will be the more impossible since they are in truth the same country and neither can compromise on its own superiority without detracting from the glory of the other.'[5] Because of the rule of the signifier over the signified, the two words 'Ladies' and 'Gentlemen', in the illustration above, constitute, by their very installation, the two doors, although, in some mythical prehistory prior to the signifier's arrival, the doors are identical. Similarly, it is not the biological given of male and female that is in question in psychoanalysis (this Mitchell herself makes quite clear), but the subject as constituted by the pre-existing signifying chain, that is, by culture, in which the subject must place himself. A biologistic reading of Freud sees only the subject already inserted into his position of blindness within that chain, and does not see the subject's placing himself or the chain as chain. The first image of the subject is then very much like the first image above, the drawing of the tree: a one-to-one correspondence is assumed between, for example, the word 'woman' and a woman. By such a reading, the only delimitable 'thing' the signifier 'woman' could possibly 'mean' is the biological female. Whence springs the whole normalizing moralism of biologistic psychology.

However, an understanding of the signifying chain does not mean that the subject can remove himself from his blind situation merely by knowing that the second rest room exists somewhere outside his field of vision. What Lacan has sketched in the above passage is a situation of desire. The register of desire is where the 'cessation of hostilities' is 'impossible'. Although one can hypothetically reconstruct a pre-linguistic, pre-cultural 'real' (positing the two doors as originally identical, the human child as naturally bisexual), this mythical prehistory cannot erase the situation of desire which is the result of the perversion of the need by the signifier's presence. An exposition of the structured articulation of need and desire will not institute an idealistically utilitarian return to the need, to the biological, to the pre-perverted 'real'. As Lacan writes, 'far from yielding to a logicizing reduction, there where it is a question of desire we find in its irreducibility to the demand the very energy that also keeps it from being collapsed back into need. To put it elliptically: that desire be articulated, precisely for that reason it is not articulable. We mean, in the discourse appropriate to it, ethical and not psychological.'[6] The demand is made within language's imaginary register, where the first model of one-to-one correspondence is presumed to operate, and, thus, the demand is assumed to be satisfiable: its signified is assumed to be delimitable. Desire is that portion of the pre-articulated need which finds itself left out of the demand—the demand being the register of ethical discourse. Of course, Lacan can indicate the marginal place of desire, but he does this in the only way possible—in psychological discourse. In ethical discourse, spoken from our place as subjects attempting to signify ourselves in the signifying chain, we are all sitting on one side of the compartment or the other: we are all subject to the blindness imposed by our seats in the compartment; there is no other way of being on the train (chain).

To date, the feminist efforts to understand and struggle against the cultural constructs of male-dominated society would have the subject consider as illusory the entire structure which makes the realms of Gentlemen and Ladies appear defined and absolute as they do in the one-to-one correlation. That effort would place the feminist as observer in some sort of floating position outside the structure, a position of omniscience. Such positioning ignores the subject's need to place himself within the signifying chain in order to be any place at all. There is no place for a 'subject', no place to be human, to make sense outside of signification, and language always has specific rules which no subject has the power to decree. Although Mitchell also maintains that the self's alienated constitution within culture is the only means of placing itself, in her 'ethical discourse'—the chapter 'The Cultural Revolution'—she falls back into the unconscious-denying, contingency-based formulations that do not greatly differ from those of the feminists whose distortions she has exposed.

It seems that Mitchell, in the end, fails to come to grips with the feminist's place (her place) as *desirer*. By containing the goals of the feminism she would supplement by psychoanalysis inside the bounds of the feminism she is interrogating, Mitchell abandons the radical subversion of the traditional notion of a self that is whole unto itself, the very subversion she is advocating through her criticism of the biologistic and reductionistic readings of Freud that have previously influenced feminism. Because desire is non-articulable in ethical discourse and because to be within the bounds of feminism, where she would locate herself, necessitates ethical discourse (prescription for action), Mitchell is trapped into making the reign of insatiable desire contingent in order to make it impeachable. If she can banish desire from ethical discourse, that discourse can be as lucid, as infallible, as the psychological theory which precedes her last chapter. Thus in that final chapter the unconscious which, by avoiding the discussion of language she has made into a repository of some vague notion of culture, is open to being understood as culture known consciously. She then ignores the unconscious as that which in lapses, dreams, etc., always manifests itself as a disrupter, a subverter of rationality and utility. Culture thus becomes external, just as the train incident is for the omniscient observer who would ignore that the signifier has forever changed the 'meaning' of the once identical doors.

In her readings of feminists, Mitchell delineates just such a trend of utopic rationalism, of 'biological wishful thinking' (p. 221); yet, when it comes down to proposing what feminists should *do*, Mitchell's solution resembles the 'legislation from our rational standpoint' (p. 349) whose inadequacies she so accurately exposes. Mitchell suggests that we demonstrate the contradictory nature of the cultural constructs inscribed into the unconscious. Yet those contradictions are the necessary result of the subject's place—as one who desires—within the signifying chain. Desire has a contradictory nature by being that which exceeds the bounds of the imaginary satisfaction available to the demand. Her inaccurate, contingent formulation of the juncture of need and desire has left her free to banish desire by showing its non-necessity. So she proposes that 'women have to organize themselves as a group to *effect a change in the basic ideology of human society.* To be *effective,* this can be no righteous challenge to the simple domination of men. . ., but a struggle based on a theory of the *social non-necessity* at this stage of development of the *laws instituted by patriarchy*' (p. 414, my italics). She goes on to state that 'when the potentialities of the complexities of capitalism. . . are released by its overthrow, new structures will gradually come to be represented in the unconscious. It is the task of feminism to insist on their birth' (p. 415). If women can 'organize themselves as a group to effect a change in the basic ideology of human society' and can 'insist on the birth' of 'new structures' in the unconscious, then somehow they transcend the non-contingent fact that human beings, subject to the unconscious, are fated not to be rational. What about the unconscious of the feminist in which, according to Mitchell's own formulations, ought to be inscribed the constructs of a patriarchal order? Are the actions of this subject not affected by the unconscious?

If the structures in the unconscious were linked to the structural fact of articulating oneself through language—whose inception is both the beginning of society in general and of the self which is culturally constituted—perhaps it would not be so easy for Mitchell to revert to a formulation that makes the unconscious as internal culture a mere reflection of an actual, historical society, if not contemporary then past. Mitchell closes the book with the following paragraph: 'It is not a question of changing (or ending) who has or how one has babies. It is a question of overthrowing patriarchy. As the end of "eternal" class conflict is visible within the contradictions of capitalism, so too, it would seem, is the swan-song of the "immortal" nature of patriarchal culture to be heard' (p. 416). Perhaps the irony signalled by the words Mitchell sets off in the oxymorons above is double-edged. For if patriarchal culture is that within which the self originally constitutes itself, it is always already there in each subject as subject. Thus how can it be overthrown if it has been necessarily internalized in everybody who could possibly act to overthrow it? If, as Mitchell has stated (pp. 394–5), the law of patriarchal culture is the law of the symbolic, the dead Father, then the living male has no better chance of acceding to that sovereign position than does the living female. The goal of a feminism infused with the Freudianism Mitchell has advocated can no longer be the overthrowing of patriarchy. One cannot kill the Father who is already dead.

Feminism must re-examine its ends in view of Lacanian psychoanalysis. It is not patriarchal culture, but the biologistic reduction of the Law of the Dead Father to the rule of the actual, living male that must be struggled against. To understand the living male's imposture, feminism must embrace a psychoanalysis that has been returned to its original audacity through an exchange with linguistic theory. *Psychoanalysis and Feminism* certainly initiates this undertaking by beginning with an effort at fidelity to Freud's discovery. Mitchell's incisive analysis of other writers reveals the distortions attendant upon those who read Freud as pre-Freudian. The tone of her analysis is one of harsh denial, the denial of similarity with those whose errors she is exposing. Yet, although she wins the battle against these writers, she is contaminated by the exchange. At the end of the book, with the proposals for the use of psychoanalysis in the overthrow of patriarchy, she takes over the position of the writers she has criticized. If, after the injection of psychoanalysis into feminism, feminism remains unchanged, what is the point of that infusion?

Perhaps the 'and' suggestive of peaceful coexistence in the title *Psychoanalysis and Feminism* betrays Mitchell's wish that psychoanalysis should not disrupt feminism as she knows it. Perhaps that is even why her discussion of Lacan/language is so insufficient. But the stronger, wiser, better feminism she would have cannot also be still the same feminism.

2 Of Phallic Proportions: Lacanian Conceit

It has become a commonplace in discussions of psychoanalysis's relation to women to make reference to the fact that Freud did not get around to writing about the 'psychical consequences' of sexual difference[1]–about the ways in which female sexuality might differ from the model of 'human' sexuality he had generated from the little boy's history–until late in his career, around 1925. Like Freud, Jacques Lacan, in the beginning, talked about subject, language and desire without specifying the sexual differentiation of his schemes. Only two of the *Écrits* (the monumental collection of his major statements from 1936 to 1966) are directed to questions of sexual difference, of the specificity of female sexuality. Both of those texts–'The Signification of the Phallus' and 'Directive Remarks for a Congress on Feminine Sexuality'[2]–were written in 1958.

These two *écrits* with special interest to feminism are separated by only one essay. The arrangement does not seem to be strictly determined by the chronology of writing or public presentation, but rather creates its own chronology of reading. The essay separating the two 1958 writings on sexual difference is a memorial to Ernest Jones, written in 1959, a commentary on Jones's 1916 article 'The Theory of Symbolism'. Jones died on 11 February 1958. The year of his death is the year Lacan undertakes work on sexual difference, work which makes explicit reference to Jones whose major disagreement with Freud centred around female sexuality and the phallus. I would like to read the memorial to Jones as the centrepiece to Lacan's 1958 texts on sexual difference. By that I mean both that Lacan's interest in the subject is the 'broad' version of a tribute to Jones, who regretted Freud's phallocentrism and neglect of female sexuality, but also that Jones's 'Theory of Symbolism' as read by Lacan contains the central question of Lacan's articulation of sexual difference.

15

In his 1916 article on symbolism, Jones writes: 'There are probably more symbols of the male organ itself than all other symbols put together.'[3] Jones continues: 'This is a totally unexpected finding. . . and is so difficult to reconcile with our sense of proportion that it needs an effort to refuse the easy escape of simply denying the facts, a feat which is greatly facilitated by the circumstance that, thanks to our education, the facts are not very accessible.' Jones has made a discovery, 'a totally unexpected finding', one he was not prepared, not educated for. He did not expect to find that symbolism is disproportionately phallic. This injustice runs counter to his 'sense of proportion', sense of the just measure, provided by his civilized, liberal, humanist 'education', and that 'education' makes it very easy, all too temptingly easy to deny such unexpected, inappropriate 'facts'. Indeed here at the very moment of stating this discovery, an 'effort', a struggle is felt as necessary to hold on to the fact, to keep it from being buried by propriety, by the liberally educated 'sense of proportion'.

The sense of 'proportion' here employed by Jones is defined by the dictionary as 'harmonious relation; balance; symmetry'. The symbolic pre-eminence of the male organ runs counter to the civilized, liberal tradition of balance between the sexes, of a fair distribution necessary for a 'harmonious relation', a successful marriage. Eleven years later when Jones presents his first paper on female sexuality, he will begin by remarking that 'there is a healthy suspicion growing that men analysts have been led to adopt an unduly phallo-centric view. . . the importance of the female organs being correspondingly underestimated'.[4] The male analyst's view is 'unduly phallo-centric'. 'Unduly', according to the dictionary, means '1. Excessively, immoderately. 2. In disregard of a legal or moral precept.' Phallocentrism seems wrong to Jones: that is, immoral by virtue of being 'excessive, immoderate', which is to say, unreconcilable with a 'sense of proportion'. The phallic disproportion brings him, in a series of three papers between 1927 and 1935, to champion the claims of an 'underestimated' female sexuality to a more balanced, more proportionate estimate. His 'sense of proportion', his spirit of fair play, will be sufficiently scandalized to provoke his only major departure from Freud's theory.

Back in 1916, when Jones first uncovered the scandalous, immoderate fact of phallocentric symbolism, he was not protesting the injustice, but struggling to hold on to a discovery which runs

so very counter to his 'education', expectations and 'sense of proportion'. Yet his fears of easy loss come true only too soon, just as
soon as he articulates that temptation to denial and escape. Immediately after the sentence where he writes 'it needs an effort to
refuse the easy escape of simply denying the facts', there is a long
quotation from Rank and Sachs, first in the original German,
then in English translation. The apparent purpose of the quotation is to offer these authors' explanation of why phallic symbols
predominate. But the quotation does not mention phallic symbols, rather it attempts to explain the prevalence of *sexual* symbols. The long quotation ends this section of the paper. The
question of the phallocentrism of symbolism is never answered,
but rather is displaced through the path of least resistance, the
'easy escape', on to a discussion of sexual symbols in general. The
imbalance is thus righted, for 'sexual' is a general term, applying
to both sexes equally, regardless of sexual difference.

Jones's article is full of discussions on the meanings of specific
phallic symbols. Indeed as Lacan points out (*Écrits*, p. 710), all
the symbols which Jones considers in his paper are phallic symbols. But the 'totally unexpected fact'–that there are 'more
symbols of the male organ itself than all other symbols put together'–is never again confronted. Indeed the shift into a discussion of the prevalence of 'sexual' symbols allows the major
scandal of the 'fact'–the sexual disharmony, imbalance, injustice
–to be lost. The direction of Jones's 'easy escape', away from phallic disproportion and disharmony between the sexes, becomes his
explicit enterprise in 1927 when he attempts to correct the phallocentrism of Freud's theory into a model of sexuality which will
not 'underestimate' women, will not be sexually unjust nor 'difficult to reconcile with our sense of proportion.'

As tempting as it might be to applaud Jones's championing the
rights of female sexuality to an equal place in psychoanalytic
theory, it is important to read his partisanship as a repetition of
his move in 1916, to read it as an escape, a denial of the 'fact' of
symbolic phallocentrism. Perhaps even to read it as a denial
(disavowal, *Verleugnung*) in the psychoanalytic sense of the term.
Verleugnung is a 'term used by Freud in the specific sense of a
mode of defense which consists in the subject's refusing to recognize the reality of a traumatic perception–most especially the
perception of the absence of the woman's penis.... The mechanism of *Verleugnung* is first described by Freud in the course of his

discussion of castration. The denial of castration is the prototype–
and perhaps even the origin–of other kinds of denials of reality.'[5]
Denial, in the psychoanalytic sense, is the refusal to recognize a
'fact', one uncovered by a 'traumatic perception', or in Jones's
terms 'a totally unexpected finding', one that runs counter to
previous conceptions of the world. *Verleugnung* is specifically a
response to the discovery of the woman's 'castration'. As many
have commented it is extremely odd, in fact unreasonable, excessive, that Freud considers the woman's castration a 'fact', even
a perceivable 'reality'. But we will momentarily leave that problem aside so as to consider another oddness which seems to respond to Freud's. It is striking that Jones's response to the discovery
of a sexual inequity in symbolism and then in psychoanalytic
theory coincides with Freud's description of a certain response to
the discovery of an inequity in the distribution of the phallus.

Jones's first article against phallocentric theory is precisely on
the subject of castration. He denies that castration is a reasonable, proportionate[6] concept for understanding female sexuality,
and proposes that castration anxiety is merely one form of a more
general anxiety, which he would call *aphanisis*, the fear of total
disappearance of *libido*. 'Aphanisis' is a term with equal application to either sex. Thus by veering the theory from castration (the
fear of phallic loss) to *aphanisis* (the fear of sexual loss), Jones
repeats the slippage in his 1916 text from phallic to sexual symbol.

That he should act out a mechanism–*Verleugnung*–Freud had
specifically delineated as a defence against castration in the very
paper where he wanted to downplay the importance of castration
would seem to suggest that the problematic of castration and its
obviously exaggerated position in Freudian theory, the very problematic of the phallocentrism of that theory, has a certain sticki-
ness, which is not to be resolved merely by recourse to one's
liberal, humanist 'sense of proportion'.

If feminism is to change a phallocentric world, phallocentrism
must be dealt with and not denied. If Jones, through his outraged
spirit of fairness, appears as woman's ally, we should beware his
faith in the harmonious relation between the sexes. Of what use is
that faith when it wants nothing more than to cover over the disharmony from which feminism arises and which it would change.
Lacan is impolite enough, ungentlemanly enough, immoderate
enough to flaunt the phallic disproportion. Nowhere is the

phallus's privilege more exposed in all its brutal outrage to any gentlemanly 'sense of proportion' than in Lacan's theory.

The discovery made and lost by Jones–the 'fact' that there are more phallic symbols than all other symbols put together–is rediscovered by Lacan, in 1958, the year Jones dies. In 'The Signification of the Phallus' Lacan states that 'the phallus is the privileged signifier' (*Écrits*, p. 692; Sheridan, p. 287). Although Jones is concerned with 'symbols' and Lacan speaks of 'signifiers', in his reading of Jones's 'Theory of Symbolism' Lacan states that 'the only notion which allows us to conceive of the symbolism of the phallus is the particularity of its function as a signifier' (*Écrits*, p. 703). It is its privilege among signifiers that determines its predominance as a symbol. Jones did not have the necessary theoretical apparatus for viewing such an 'unexpected fact'. What Jones lacks and needs, according to Lacan, in order to have a truly psychoanalytic, non-mystical theory of symbolism, is modern (that is, post-Saussurean) linguistic theory, as well as a notion of the rule of the signifier over the speaking subject.

Jones discovered that only a small number of 'ideas' are ever symbolized: 'ideas of the self and the immediate blood relatives, or of the phenomena of birth, love, and death' (Jones, *The Theory of Symbolism*, p. 102). Lacan says of these 'ideas' that they 'designate the points where the subject disappears under the being of the signifier; whether in effect it is a question of being oneself, being a father, being born, being loved or being dead, how can one not see that the subject, if he is the subject who speaks, can only sustain himself there through discourse' (*Écrits*, p. 709). What Jones continues to try to understand as 'ideas'–thus expecting a sense of their logic, their reasonableness, their general application–Lacan sees as the points where the domination of the signifier–the external, material letter of language–over any individual speaking subject is critical, oppressive and even deadly. The signifier has 'being', is materially present and enduring, whereas the subject 'disappears', lacks being. Lacan's 'disappearance of the subject' is reminiscent of Jones's *aphanisis*–itself the Greek word for 'disappearance'–a term to which Lacan makes respectful reference in 'The Signification of the Phallus'. But Lacan prefers to retain the Freudian term 'castration', which he uses to refer to the subject's relation to the signifier.

Why does Lacan insist upon using the phallic, sexually unreasonable, unbalanced term 'castration' for the general relation of

subject to signifier? This question rejoins Jones's unexpected discovery of the phallocentrism of symbols, and his reaction to that
discovery. Lacan refuses to use a generalizable, sexually indifferent term like *aphanisis*, and retains a term which unveils the
obscene privilege of the phallus.

According to Lacan, the phallus is 'the signifier intended to
designate as a whole the effects of signified, in that the signifier
conditions them by its presence as signifier' (*Écrits*, p. 690;
Sheridan, p. 285). It is glaringly disproportionate for one particular signifier to 'designate' the whole of the effects of signification. By what right does this part, this portion signify, represent
the whole? 'Our sense of proportion' cannot accept this usurpa-
tion. *Pro-portion* is etymologically 'for the portion', in favour of
the part, on the part's side rather than the whole's. The etymology
of 'proportion' then leads us to 'disproportion', one portion
having a disproportionate share. The part for the whole is a
common definition of the rhetorical figure metonymy. But this
definition is itself metonymical, since 'the part for the whole' is
only one kind, one portion of metonymy. This definition is in-
correct; yet more general definitions tend to be vague and confusing, difficult to grasp or remember, which contributes to the
persistence of the partial definition. Metonymy resists a general
definition, one that would be meta-metonymical, and the metonymical definition—illustration remains, although marked as in-
complete, partial, the part for the whole.

In 1957, a year before 'The Signification of the Phallus', Lacan
writes that 'desire *is* a metonymy' (*Écrits*, p. 528; Sheridan, p.
175). Lacan ends 'The Signification of the Phallus' by insisting,
contrary to our sense of fair play, that desire, the Freudian libido,
is masculine. Metonymy is a phallic conceit, the part standing for
the whole, standing for the hole. The substitution of the phallus
(one sexual part) for the whole of sexuality is an example of
metonymy, not what it should be (metonymy properly should
have a varied definition with many sorts of relations), but what it
stubbornly insists upon being (continually misconstrued as the
part for the whole).[7]

Jones's 'sense of proportion' has led us into the heart of conceits
whence springs Lacan's phallus. It is as if Jones's 1916 moment of
discovery, moment of truth, although immediately denied and
lost, imprinted itself in the very letter of his text, which according
to Lacan is where the truth appears—not in thoughts, but in

things, not in the spirit, but in the material, contingent letter.[8]

All this keeps returning to the same offensive 'fact': that the phallus has unreasonable privilege. It is difficult not to want to dismiss and bury something so unreasonable, not at least to demand from the phallus a reason for its rule. One asks for 'the reason', the idea, the cause behind the signifier, but what one gets is 'la raison', a specific signifier in a given language, in this case French. Lacan writes: 'the phallus as signifier gives *la raison* of desire (in the sense in which the term is used in music in the "mean and extreme *raison*" of harmonic division)' (*Écrits*, p. 693; Sheridan, p. 288). 'Raison' besides carrying the various senses of its cognate 'reason' has a particular mathematical and musical sense: it means 'proportion'. Through the contingencies of a specific signifier–'raison'–one can ask for a reason and get a proportion. All this contingent, marginal word-play seems to be at the very conceited heart of Lacan's text, and of our concern here which is the unreasonable, disproportionate rule of the signifier (the dead, alien, stubborn material which is the necessary and inevitable support for a concrete discourse, an act of speaking) over the subject.

Our education and its underlying ideology make it 'an effort to refuse the easy escape' when it comes to facing a disharmony, a disproportion, what might be called a class conflict. The liberal, humanist tradition which always threatens to re-cover our discoveries of obscene truths makes the recognition of 'castration', of a certain unfair distribution between men and women, subject to revision in the direction of complementarity and symmetry. This liberal, humanist ideology is not just external to us, but is our very ego. The ego is the psychic agency responsible for revision, in the psychoanalytic sense. 'Secondary revision' is 'the rearrangement of a dream so as to present it in the form of a relatively consistent and comprehensible scenario'.[9] According to Lacan, Freud discovered that the way to undo secondary revision is to pay attention to whatever remains of the eccentricity of the material of the dream, of the letter of the text. Thus the feminist struggle to confront phallic disproportion must be that 'effort to refuse the easy escape' which Jones recognized as 'necessary' but was not equal to, the effort to concentrate on the 'fact', on the letter, as disproportionate as its importance might seem, precisely because of its unreasonable proportions.

Jones looked for a reason (*une raison*) for the 'totally unexpected fact' and Lacan finds that the phallus is the 'mean and extreme *raison* [ratio]'–which means 'a proportion in which a whole is to one of its parts as that one is to the second'. In question here is some 'whole' which is made up of two parts, like humanity is divided into two sexes. The phallus is both the (dis)proportion between the sexes, and the (dis)proportion between any sexed being by virtue of being sexed (having parts, being partial) and human totality. So the man is 'castrated' by not being total, just as the woman is 'castrated' by not being a man. Whatever relation of lack man feels, lack of wholeness, lack in/of being,[10] is projected onto woman's lack of phallus, lack of maleness. Woman is then the figuration of phallic 'lack'; she is a hole. By these mean and extreme phallic proportions, the whole is to man as man is to the hole.

The accidental play of homonymy gives us a chiasmus ('a rhetorical inversion of the second of two parallel structures'), which by depending upon the letter, the signifier, seems to offer up an uncanny truth. For the 'whole' in relation to which man is lacking, has its basis in what in Freudian terms is called the 'phallic mother'. The 'whole' is the pre-Oedipal mother, apparently omnipotent and omniscient, until the 'discovery of her castration', the discovery that she is not a 'whole', but a 'hole'. So the woman (phallic mother) is to the man what the man is to the (castrated) woman. It is not that men and women are simply unequal, but they occupy the same position in different harmonic ratios, at different moments. The effect is a staggering of position. As Freud said, 'one gets an impression that a man's love and a woman's are a phase apart psychologically'.[11]

The skewing of man and woman, the 'phase apart psychologically', is bodied forth in the structure of Lacan's 'Signification of the Phallus'. On the first page of that text, Lacan presents a series of three elements, which I would like to put into correspondence with the three 'parts' (whole and its two portions) of the 'mean and extreme ratio'. He writes: 'the unconscious castration complex has the function of a knot...in...the installation in the subject of an unconscious position without which he would be unable to identify himself with the ideal type of his sex, or to respond without grave risk to the needs of his partner in the sexual relation, *voire* [or even] to receive in a satisfactory way the needs of the child that is procreated in this relation' (*Écrits*, p. 685; Sheridan, p. 281).

The first element—'identify with the ideal type of his sex'—is the necessary task of either sex, presented in a manner which makes that task separate but equal, like Jones's *aphanisis* and 'sexual' symbols. Sheridan translates the French 'il' and 'son' with the masculine English pronouns. The French word for subject is masculine, in that language which has no neuter nouns. Simply to translate with the currently used balanced locutions 'he/she' or 'she/he' would not solve this problem, because as the series progresses the sexual differentiation of the subject becomes the problem, which any consistent and balanced pronoun might obscure. Also: the accidental fact that 'subject' is a masculine noun is consistent with Lacan's theory, which articulates the constitution of any subject in masculine or, if one prefers, phallic terms and makes evident the problematic relation of any female subject to language, to the very language, the very arbitrary laws, that constitute 'sujet' as masculine.

The second element—'respond to the needs of his partner in the sexual relation'—would seem in line with the male role. If the man has not satisfactorily resolved his castration complex, he may be impotent or otherwise incapable of vaginal penetration or vaginal ejaculation, and thus be unable to 'respond to his partner's needs'. The word Lacan chooses is 'needs' not 'desires' or 'demands' and thus refers more to the biological sexual function (that is, the reproductive function) than to the sexuality which Freud theorized as always exceeding and perverting the reproductive function. On the other hand, a frigid woman, even a raped woman, regardless of her neuroses, is more likely than a sexually dysfunctional man to be able to satisfy the biological, reproductive 'needs' of her partner. So it seems that, unlike 'sexual identification', this second element is suitable to the masculine pronoun 'his'.

The third element—'receive the needs of the child'—seems to be of more concern to the female role. It is the woman, generally, whose role it is to take care of the child's needs (again we are in the register of the real, the biological—the father may be necessary to the child in the register of language, of desire). The third element is conjoined to the second by the word 'voire', which Sheridan translates as 'or even'.

The distinction we are making between the male role which deals with the partner, and the female role which concerns itself with the child is taken from Freud's *Civilization and its Discon-*

tents. He writes that when the need for genital satisfaction was no longer periodic as it is in other mammals 'the male acquired a motive for keeping the female... near him; while the female, who did not want to be separated from her helpless young, was obliged, in their interests, to remain with the stronger male'.[12] The man wants to be with his woman; the woman stays 'for the sake of the children'. This is not a balanced, symmetrical dual relation, but one of three parties. The child is to the woman what the woman is to the man. The reciprocity is skewed. A few years after writing *Civilization and its Discontents* Freud will say: 'How often it happens... that it is only his son who obtains what he himself aspired to: one gets an impression that a man's love and a woman's are a phase apart psychologically' ('Femininity', loc. cit.).

The reading I have done so far of Lacan's sentence with its three-part series seems forced and arbitrary. It is the paragraph following the sentence we have just read which confers the signification I am discussing. It is in this next paragraph that Lacan makes reference to *Civilization and its Discontents.* That reference leads us to the Freud quotation which shaped our distinction between male and female role. The first sentence in the paragraph, the sentence immediately following the one we just were reading, also has three parts; and, more strikingly, the word 'voire', a relatively unusual adverb, appears in both sentences between the second and third part. This repetition gives 'voire' an insistence, an importance which such a marginal word is not expected to have, and which is totally lost in the translation.

Lacan's next sentence reads: 'There is an antinomy, here, that is internal to the assumption by man (*Mensch*) of his sex: why must he assume the attributes of that sex only through a threat, *voire* [or even] through the aspect of a privation?' I have altered Sheridan's translation in order to restore the 'voire', and its position conjoining the two sexes in their different relations to castration. Sheridan translates: 'Why must he assume the attributes of that sex only through a threat—the threat, indeed of their privation?' By not translating 'voire' by the same locution in both sentences Sheridan obscures the similarity in structure between the two sentences. The first time 'voire' occurs Sheridan translates it as 'or even'. 'Voire' distinguishes between two elements, with the implication that the one introduced by 'voire' is similar to the one preceding it, but more far-fetched. In this case if castration is a contradictory way for man to assume his sex, it is even more far-fetched in relation to woman. Besides losing the repetition of 'voire', Sheridan condenses the 'threat' and the 'privation' into the 'threat of privation'. But Freud's sexually differentiated reading sees the threat of castration as the male version of the complex, whereas privation is the woman's story. She is under no threat; she has been deprived of a phallus. In fact, the paragraph beginning with this sentence ends with a mention of 'the castration complex in the masculine unconscious and . . . *penisneid* in the unconscious of woman'. *Penisneid* (penis-envy) is the female version of the castration complex, experienced not as a threat but as a privation. Sheridan's obliteration of the conjunction 'voire' has effaced sexual difference in its relation to castration and to sexual identities, effacing the woman's castration, denying castration itself at the very moment the text he is translating is discussing it.

In this second sentence the relation between the series of three and sexual differentiation is more obvious than in the first sentence. The first element is once again the whole of humanity, the generality which is marked by the intrusion of the German word 'Mensch'. The appearance of 'Mensch' marks that in the first part of the sentence we are speaking of men and women together in this sexually undifferentiated word, concerned with the whole before it divides into its two parts, actually with the whole at the moment it divides into its two parts. The translation of 'his sex' poses a different problem than in the previous sentence, despite the fact that 'homme' is a masculine noun. Perhaps here it might be effective to translate 'son' as 'his/her' since the intrusion of the German word already constitutes this as a place where the problems of sexual difference as posed in translation are explicit. The use of the German word reminds the reader that sexual identity is always assumed within a given language with its own laws. Passing from one language to another is a way of making the arbitrariness of that identity visible.

Both sentences, as I have tried to show, scan into three elements: the first inclusive of both sexes, the second male, the third female. As soon as the general question of assumption of sexual identity is broached (the topic of the first element in both sentences: 'identify himself with the ideal type of his sex' and 'assumption by man (*Mensch*) of his sex'), the path of that assumed identity must bifurcate. Separate consideration must be given to man and woman.

The 'mean and extreme ratio' can be seen more obviously in

the second sentence we are considering. The antinomy, which is 'internal' in the first element, between man's assuming his sex and his castration/loss of sex (in other words, between being a male sexed being and being whole, a *Mensch*, a phallic mother) is repeated in the antinomy marked by the conjunction 'voire' between being threatened by castration (thus still phallic, if fragilely so) and being 'castrated', phallically deprived, a woman.

After the second three-part sentence Lacan continues thus: 'In "Civilization and its Discontents" Freud, as we know, went so far as to suggest a disturbance of human sexuality, not of a contingent, but of an essential kind.' Sheridan's translation, his revision/suppression of the impact of 'voire', would leave us with that disturbance simply being a general inadequation between human desire and satisfaction, the general human 'fact of castration'. This is usually understood to be the thesis of *Civilization and its Discontents*. But our discovery of a second antinomy, a disturbance *between* the sexes, corresponds to the sentence quoted above from *Civilization and its Discontents* in which the man wants the woman and the woman wants the child.

This sentence about the woman staying with the man 'for the sake of the children' is a real locus of trouble in *Civilization and its Discontents*. Right at the end of this sentence appears a disturbingly long footnote (over a page in length) which does not seem to relate directly to the sentence (pp. 99–100). The footnote discusses at length and in extended and tangential detail the depreciation of olfactory sexual stimuli and their replacement by visual sexual stimuli. The oddness of such a long footnote is only amplified by another even longer footnote on the same subject at the end of this same chapter. That second footnote begins by talking about the difference between masculine and feminine (the subject of the sentence in the text at the point of the first footnote) and then progresses to a detailed discussion of the devaluation of the olfactory. Both footnotes in their excess signal a trouble which is not the 'discontent' thematized by the book (general sexual discontent) but which is located at the intersection of sexual difference and the difference between the senses of smell and sight.

How resonant then that the insistent word which Lacan places twice at the juncture between male and female identity is 'voire', an exact homonym for 'voir', which means to see. Again it seems the contingencies of the signifier produce an effective signification. In the castration complex, between the male and the female is a 'voire', but also a 'voir', an act of seeing. Freud articulates the 'discovery of castration' around a sight: sight of a phallic presence in the boy, sight of a phallic absence in the girl, ultimately sight of a phallic absence in the mother. Sexual difference takes its actual divisive significance upon a sighting. The privilege of the phallus as presence, the concomitant 'disappearance' of any female genitalia under the phallic order, is based on the privilege of sight over other senses. The penis, according to Freud, is more visible than what the little girl has. From being more visible, it becomes simply more, in other words better, superior.

Yet in the two disturbing footnotes to *Civilization and its Discontents* Freud links this privilege of sight to the degradation of smell, and ties the whole problematic to sexual difference. Perhaps smell has a privileged relation to female sexuality. According to Freud, before the triumph of the eye over the nose, 'the menstrual process produced an effect on the male psyche by means of olfactory stimuli' (p. 99, note). The penis may be more visible, but female genitalia have a stronger smell.

This connection between the feminine and the olfactory leads me to a statement made by Michèle Montrelay in her review of the book *Female Sexuality: New Psychoanalytic Views*: 'this book... lets femininity speak in an *immediate* mode that one can never forget. From it emanates an "odor di femina".'[13] Montrelay's review of *Female Sexuality*–taking as its point of departure the 'Freud–Jones quarrel'–spins out the clearest and yet most subtle elaboration of Lacanian theory on sexual difference, and specifically on female sexuality, that exists.

According to Montrelay, the unbearably intense immediacy of the 'odor di femina' produces anxiety, a state totally threatening to the stability of the psychic economy, that stability which is achieved by means of representations. The visual mode produces representations as a way of mastering what is otherwise too intense. The 'odor di femina' becomes odious, nauseous, because it threatens to undo the achievements of repression and sublimation, threatens to return the subject to the powerlessness, intensity and anxiety of an immediate, unmediated connection with the body of the mother.

This distinction between a more immediate, primitive, olfactory sexuality and a mediated, sublimated, visual sexuality can be found in those odd footnotes to *Civilization and its Discon-*

tents. The fact that the first economy is odious because it under-mines the difficultly achieved control of the second economy can also be traced back to Freud's musing on the subject. Freud writes: 'the taboo on menstruation [source of the most powerful 'odor di femina'] is derived from this "organic repression" [repression of the olfactory in favour of the visual], as a defence against a phase of development that has been surmounted' (*Civilization and its Discontents*, p. 99). Montrelay considers the second economy (mediation, representation), as an advance over the first. She considers sublimation to be positive and necessary for con-taining anxiety and making life livable. Sublimation is not de-sexualization, she specifies, but a more mediated, represented, mastered form of sexuality.

In the second of his smelly footnotes, Freud writes that 'with the depreciation of his sense of smell, it was not only [man's] anal erotism which threatened to fall a victim to organic repression, but the whole of his sexuality; so that since this, the sexual func-tion has been accompanied by a repugnance which cannot further be accounted for, and which prevents its complete satisfaction and forces it away from the sexual aim into sublimations and libidinal displacements' (op. cit., p. 106). The devaluation of the olfactory leads into 'sublimations and libidinal displacements' and away from 'complete satisfaction'. This is Lacanian 'castra-tion'–the sacrifice of 'complete satisfaction', a sacrifice necessary to adult sexuality, to assume sexual identity. According to Lacan 'displacement' is metonymy (*Écrits*, p. 511; Sheridan, p. 160), and 'desire *is* a metonymy (*Écrits*, p. 528; Sheridan, p. 175). Thus this absence of 'complete satisfaction' coupled with 'displace-ments' characterizes what Lacan calls desire. Desire, Lacan says, is excentric (*excentré–Écrits*, p. 690; Sheridan, p. 286). 'Excen-tré' means 'having a displaced centre', which is to say in Freud's words, 'forced away from the aim and into displacements'.

Unlike 'desire', unlike Freudian masculine libido, feminine sexuality is *not* subject to metonymy, mediation and sublimation. Desire may always be masculine, but not sexuality. If the sexuality of desire (mediated, sublimated) is *phallocentric*, if desire is *eccentric*, feminine sexuality (immediate, olfactory) is, according to Montrelay, *concentric*. Montrelay borrows the term 'concentri-que' from Béla Grunberger's paper in *Female Sexuality* where Grunberger writes: 'we said that singleness is the mark of narciss-ism and, indeed, there is a *concentric* aspect characteristic of woman's libidinal cathexis; she is always at the center of it, but at the same time the center is the phallus which is also essentially unique'.[14] Although Grunberger uses and even italicizes the term 'concentric', it does not yet seem to have the shape Montrelay will give it. For Grunberger 'concentric' is ultimately 'phallocentric': 'but at the same time the center is the phallus'. Beyond even Grunberger's specific articulation, it may be that 'centric' of any sort is always phallic. After all, 'centric' derives from the Greek word *kentrein* meaning 'to prick'.

It is the insistence of the letter, put into relief by Montrelay, that offers us this new way of reading phallocentrism. By bringing together the terms 'phallocentrique' and 'concentrique', she makes one hear the 'con' which, overdetermined by its parallel position with the already genital 'phallo', brings out the cunt in concentric. Yet once one starts attending to the odd truths revealed in the accidental material of language, one is led into a different kind of reading, no longer a sublimated relation to the spirit of the text, but an intercourse with its body, so that the scientific Latino-Greek term 'concentric' reveals its stunning vulgarity as a 'cunt-prick'.

While both phallocentric and concentric are centred organizations, 'eccentric', Lacan's term for desire, is a decentred organization. Phallic Lacanian desire is always a displacement of the phallic centre. Lacan writes that the phallus 'can play its role only when veiled' (*Écrits*, p. 692; Sheridan, p. 288). The 'prick' at the centre of phallocentrism unveils the phallus and spoils its game. It is the ec-centricity of desire, the avoidance of the centre, of the 'prick', which keeps the phallus its privilege as signifier. A sexuality which would remain at the centre, whether that centre be a vagina or a penis, would no longer be phallic, no longer promote the privilege of the veiled phallus.

Whereas Montrelay uses the term 'concentric' to speak of feminine sexuality, playing up its parallelism with phallocentric, Lacan uses the word 'contiguity'. In 'Directive Remarks' he says that 'feminine sexuality appears as the effort of a *jouissance* enveloped in its own *contiguité. . . to realize itself in rivalry* with the desire that castration liberates in the male' (*Écrits*, p. 735). 'Jouissance' is frequently cited by translators as an untranslatable word, one that will tolerate no mediation but must be present in the text and not displaced into another language's 'equivalent'. It means enjoyment, also orgasm, and tends to be linked to a loss of control, a more primitive experience than the words 'plaisir' (pleasure) and 'orgasme'. Montrelay contrasts a sublimated phallocentric orgasm with unmediated, concentric *jouissance*. You can have one or multiple orgasms; they are quantifiable, delimitable. You cannot have one 'jouissance' and there is no plural. Feminine sexuality, the alternative, the rival to (always masculine) desire is characterized by contiguity. The 'con' is still present as in concentric, but the centre, the *kentrein*, the 'prick' is absent. No longer parallel with a phallocentric economy, 'contiguity' is more radically other. 'Contiguous' means 'touching, nearby, adjacent'. Feminine sexuality, unlike the mediation of the visible which sustains phallic desire, is of the register of touching, nearness, presence, immediacy, contact.

The register of contiguity is where the linguist Roman Jakobson, and Lacan who borrows the term from him, situate metonymy. Metonymy is the relation between contiguous signifiers, whereas metaphor is the relation between possible equivalents, only one present in any given concrete discourse. The metonymical dimension follows the linear progression of language, one signifier articulated at a time.[15] Since any signifier can receive signification by deferred action, after the fact, no signification is ever closed, ever satisfied. For example, words at the beginning of a sentence receive signification from words later in the sentence. Since words elicit a desire for meaning, there is a drive to complete the sentence, fully reveal the signification. Yet any 'sentence' can always be added to; no sentence is ever completely saturated. The play of metonymy, the forward push to finish signification, to close meaning, creates the impression of veiled signification which Lacan links to the symbolism of the phallus.

Since for Lacan 'desire is a metonymy', it operates in the register of contiguity. Thus it appears that in Lacan's writings both feminine sexuality and masculine desire have a relation to contiguity. Perhaps this folding back in of two 'opposites' should remind us that feminine sexuality is not the complement but the supplement of desire. The 'rivalry' between the two is possible because both operate in the same dimension, the metonymical. The difference is that desire is metonymical impatience, anticipation pressing ever forward along the line of discourse so as to close signification, whereas feminine sexuality is a *'jouissance* enveloped in its own contiguity'. Such *jouissance* would be sparks of pleasure ignited by *contact* at any point, any moment along the line, not waiting for a closure, but enjoying the touching. As a result of such sparks, the impatient economy aimed at finished meaning-products (theses, conclusions, definitive statements) might just go up in smoke.

There are moments in both Montrelay's and Lacan's texts when the syllable 'con', sometimes spelled 'com', repeats with a frequency which contaminates the usually phallic, mediated, veiled language with a bodily presence, an evocative 'odor di femina'. Although the words are 'intended' to have other significations, to lead us ever forward metonymically to some possible closure, definitive statement, conclusion of the argument, the insistent 'con', the display of cunts gives us an immediate contact with the language.

The following are two examples of such an immediate presence, necessarily accompanied by our awkward recognition of the untranslatability of such odoriferous presences—the texts becoming more vulgar, more vulvar in translation:

In order to reassure [man], to *cuntvince* him, woman advances even further along the path that is hers: she explains herself, she wants to speak the truth, without *cuntprehending* [understanding] that her discourse is inadmissible. For precisely the fact of *saying* everything, that is to say, of going beyond the law of repression, *cuntaminates* the most precious truth, renders it suspect, odious, *cuntdemnable.* (Montrelay, *L'Ombre et le nom,* p. 72)

Is it this privilege of the signifier that Freud is aiming at by suggesting that there is perhaps only one libido and that it is marked with the male sign? If some chemical *cuntfiguration* sustained it beyond, could one not see there the exalting *cuntjunction* of the dissymmetry of molecules, used in living *cuntstruction,* with the lack *cuntcerted* in the subject by language, in order that there can be exercised here a rivalry between the defenders of desire and the appelants of *le sexe.* (Lacan, *Écrits,* pp. 735–6)

Montrelay's passage on the inadmissibility of woman's discourse is itself an example of such condemnable talk. Contrary to phallic veiling, feminine discourse reveals the sex organ. The presence of the cunt is equally concerted in Lacan. It appears at the very moment when he states the privilege of the phallus. The rivalry between the sexes, rivalry between 'le sexe' (common French euphemism for 'woman' as well as the term for the genitals of either sex) and desire (always male), takes place in the text. The 'appelants of *le sexe*' are the parties bringing an appeal against a legal decree (against phallic, patriarchal law, unjust to 'le sexe') but also the 'namers of *le sexe*'. The French legal term 'appelant' is the present participle of the verb 'appeler', to call by name. In this sense, 'appelant du sexe' would be someone who spoke the sex organ's name (even woman's name), in this case 'con'. At the very moment in Lacan's text when phallic privilege is asserted, the cunt clamours for recognition, makes a big stink.

After the 'big stink', Lacan has nothing left to assert about feminine sexuality or the phallus, his phallic privilege is momentarily burnt out by the sparks of *jouissance*. The 'Directive Remarks' offer nothing more save a few questions. Those cunts gaping in the preceding paragraph were just so many holes in the text, and Lacan ends not by plugging up those holes, but by maintaining them as questions. This may be a truly feminist gesture, to end with questions, not to conclude, but to be open. It is worth noting that Lacan arrives at this 'feminist gesture' by passing through an assertion of the phallus's privilege which provokes the cunt's appealing (appelant) clamour. Rather than deny the 'fact' of phallic privilege, Lacan flaunts it. And that just may be the path to accede to some sort of place for feminine sexuality to manifest itself.

3 The Ladies' Man

In 1974, the journal *L'Arc*, which devotes each of its issues to an important figure on the Paris artistic-intellectual scene, published an issue on Lacan. That *Arc, L'Arc* 58, is both the Lacan issue and an issue to which all the contributors are women. For some time now, it has been a popular feminist tactic for women to take over the direction of some review and bring forth a special women's issue. What is unusual, in this case, is that the women gave birth to a women's issue which is at the same time the Lacan issue. By what right does Lacan's portrait grace the cover of *L'Arc*'s women's issue?

A real ladies' man, there is nothing he wants more than to be with the women. Lacan, who rarely delineates his divergence from Freud, is proud to make one distinction clear. In his seminar of 13 March 1973, he says 'What I approach this year is what Freud expressly left aside, the *Was will das Weib?* the *What does Woman want?*'[1]

Lacan's seminar for that year, 1972–3, is centred upon the lecture given on 20 February, entitled 'Dieu et la jouissance de femme'. The definite article before 'femme' is crossed out, *barré* (as he puts it), because woman is that which exceeds any attempt at universalization. I say that the year is centred upon 20 February, because that is literally the centre of the book, the midpoint of the lectures, as well as the moment when Lacan discusses Bernini's Saint Teresa which appears on the cover of the published *Séminaire livre XX*. On 20 February, Lacan's purpose is to hazard cautiously some remarks about 'the other satisfaction, that which responds to phallic pleasure'. Lacan is with the women to try to get at their response.

That lecture on 20 February begins with Lacan saying 'For a long time now I have desired to speak to you while strolling a bit among you. I also hoped, I can certainly admit it to you, that the so-called school holidays would have *éclairci* [clarified, enlightened, made lighter, made thinner] your attendance' (p. 61). He desires to stroll through the audience in order to shed some light on this silent 'dark continent': to ask the question Freud avoided, '*Was will das Weib?*' Lacan derives a phallic enjoyment from his lectures, where everyone adoringly takes down his every word as if it were The Word, the Logos which has a phallic fullness, self-sufficiency. Yet Lacan would talk from the audience, 'with the women', in an attempt to get at the other enjoyment, that which responds to the phallic.

This satisfaction is refused him. He cannot talk from the audience. He cannot talk and at the same time be in the audience. Yet that is his longstanding desire. He wants to be with the women, but as the ladies' man. He wants to take that stroll as the cock of the walk.

The cock is that which by definition cannot be with the women. The seminar of 1972–3 states that over and over again. In the opening lecture of the year, Lacan declares that 'Phallic pleasure [*jouissance*] is the obstacle through which man does not succeed...in taking possession of and revelling in [*jouir de*] the woman's body, precisely because he takes possession of and revels in [*jouit de*] the organ's pleasure' (p. 13). Inasmuch as he proclaims this throughout the year, he is, in a way, with the women. Feminists could find little to argue with in this statement and its various correlates. Throughout the year's lectures, the phallic order and phallic enjoyment are shown to be a kind of failure: a failure to reach the Other, a short-circuiting of desire by which it turns back upon itself. The phallic order fails because, although unable to account for the feminine, it would, none the less, operate as a closure, attempting to create a closed universe that is thoroughly phallocentric. The sexual relation as relation between the sexes fails. This topic of the necessary impotence of the phallic, appearing throughout the twentieth seminar, is in keeping with feminist analyses of the workings and shortcomings of phallocentrism. So Lacan, who can't strut among the women, joins the women in his analysis of the failure of his desire.

Still, however, he craves that response; he desires to provoke 'the other satisfaction, that which responds to phallic pleasure'. In the same lecture that begins with his wish to get a feel for the audience, Lacan complains that 'since the time that we've been begging women, begging them on bended knee, to try to tell us something about this other pleasure, well then, not a word! We've never succeeded in getting anything out of them.' Gallantly on his knees to pop the question, Lacan in his entire seminar asks but one thing: *Was will das Weib?*

He gets an answer. The title of this twentieth seminar is the tauntingly ambivalent answer: *Encore.* On 20 February Lacan says of Saint Teresa: 'you have only to go and look at the Bernini statue in Rome to understand immediately that she's coming, no doubt about it'. Saint Teresa's ecstasy responds to the phallic, and on the cover of the twentieth seminar, just above the statue's head is the year's title, *Encore,* placed there like a cartoon dialogue balloon. That title appears to issue forth from the parted lips of the ecstatic mystic. The woman—the audience—cries 'encore'; her desire is never sated. That's precisely what frightened Freud. 'Encore' calls both for a repetition of the phallic performance, and for more, for something else. Lacan knows 'Encore' calls for something else, something he jokingly refers to as 'beyond the phallus', but he cannot help but want to give an 'encore', another phallic performance. He wants to stroll among the audience, among the women, but he wants to be cock of the walk.

Lacan declares on that 20 February that 'There is a pleasure [*jouissance*]...an enjoyment of the body, which is...(why not make a book title out of it?...) *beyond the phallus*. That would be really cute' (p. 69). Here we have the statement of feminist principle, simultaneously undercut by the Nietzsche–Freud parody ('*Beyond*...'), as well as the 'That would be really cute.'

Shoshana Felman in her contribution to *L'Arc,* 58–'La Méprise et sa chance'–distinguishes between Lacan and contemporary French 'deconstructive' philosophy on the grounds that philosophy, no matter how deconstructive, remains 'discursive', whereas Lacan's writing is 'poetic': allusive, contradictory. The ladies' man is an expert at flirtation. Unlike the man's man, philosopher or hunter, who spends his time with serious, frank confrontations, the ladies' man is always embroiled in coquetry: his words necessarily and erotically ambiguous. The ladies' man is looked at askance by the 'real man' who suspects the flirt of effeminacy.

Feminists have been hard on the ladies' man, presuming that his intentions are strictly dishonourable. They're right. But should not feminism be working to undo the reign of honour, and all those virile virtues? Inasmuch as feminists are hard on anyone, they betray an inappropriate (which is to say, all too appropriate and proper) phallicization.

Lacan is not always seductive and elusive. His coy flirtation continually tends to freeze into a rigid system centred upon the phallus as transcendental signifier. His discourse presents an alternation between a reading of 'Encore' as a call for something more, something else, something beyond, and a reading of 'Encore' as a request for the same old phallic performance.

But it is when 'encore' means 'repeat the question', which will only be answered by another 'encore', that the phallic order is most effectively threatened. Any conclusive answer to 'What does Woman want?' is an effort to recuperate the question back into the closure. It is the continual asking of it as an open question that makes the closure impossible to maintain.

Lacan asks the question. And never remains long satisfied with recuperative answers. He keeps asking 'What does Woman want, anyway?' because that is the only thing a ladies' man really needs to know.

It seems paradoxical that at the moment of *L'Arc* 58, the moment Lacan is with the women, accusations have begun to be heard from many quarters that Lacan is phallocentric. Not only do feminists decry his privileging of the phallus in his system, but 'deconstructive' philosophers—most prominently Jacques Derrida—are denouncing Lacan's phallocentrism.[2] Derrida is approaching the proper epithet, but misfiring by virtue of adherence to polite, discursive, philosophical terms that fall short of the scandal in Lacan's position. It is too eloquent, too comfortable, too complicitous with philosophical mastery, simply to claim that Lacan is phallocentric. Lacan's practice, in so far as it is traversed by resistances to metaphysical discourse and by irruptions against Oedipal paternalism, is only accessible in an earthier, less categorial discourse, attuned to the register of aggression and desire. Not simply a philosopher, but, artfully, a performer, he is no mere father figure out to purvey the truth of his authority; he also comes out seeking his pleasure in a relation that the phallocentric universe does not circumscribe. To designate Lacan at his most stimulating and forceful is to call him something more than just phallocentric. He is also phallo-eccentric. Or, in more pointed language, he is a prick.

Unlike (although related to) phallocentrism, which women resent on principle, the prick is both resented by and attractive to women. In vulgar (non-philosophical) usage, the 'prick' is both the male sexual organ (the famous penis of penis-envy: attraction—resentment) and an obnoxious person—an unprincipled and selfish man who high-handedly abuses others, who capriciously exhibits little or no regard for justice. Usually restricted to men, this epithet astoundingly often describes someone whom women (or men who feel the 'prick' of this man's power, men in a non-phallic position), despite themselves, find irresistible.

Lacan, who in his seminars constantly belittles and insults his audience, has no trouble filling a huge hall with people who adoringly write his pronouncements down word for word, since who would dare to 'take notes' on Lacan's lecture as if one could presume to know what was most important. In her introduction to *L'Arc* 58, Catherine Clément writes of Lacan's seminars: 'One understood nothing, if by understanding is meant the discursive exposition of arguments which one had been taught to practice. Nothing, for several years; but a familiarity began to form in the ear, by necessity, nonetheless' ('Un numéro' *L'Arc*, 58, p. 2). Why would anyone listen for several years to something she could not understand?

Jacqueline Rousseau-Dujardin, in her contribution to *L'Arc* 58, makes a similar confession. She first tried to attend Lacan's seminars in the early years at Saint-Anne, and although she says that 'what was said passed, *hélas!* resolutely over my head' ('Du temps qu'entends-je?', *L'Arc*, 58, p. 33), returned to the seminars later at the École Normale, enthusiastically read the *Écrits* when they appeared, and now ventures to publish an article on Lacan in which she admits (proudly, of course) that 'it is risky to write on Lacan' (p. 34). To declare something 'over my head' is commonly an aggressive way to dismiss it as effete and unnecessarily abstruse. Yet in this case it is obviously not a dismissal, but a public self-deprecation. Why would anyone subject herself to this sort of beating?

Unlike phallocentrism which locates itself in a clear-cut polemic field where opposition conditions a certain good and evil, the prick is 'beyond good and evil', 'beyond the phallus'. Phallocentrism and the polemic are masculine, upright matters. The prick, in some crazy way, is feminine.

The prick does not play by the rules; he (she) is a narcissistic tease who persuades by means of attraction and resistance, not by orderly systematic discourse. The prick, which as male organ might be expected to epitomize masculinity, lays bare its desire. Since the phallic order demands that the law rather than desire issue from the paternal position, an exposure of the father as desiring, a view of the father as prick, a view of the father's prick, feminizes him. Lacan, inasmuch as he acts gratuitously nasty, betrays his sexualized relation to his listeners. The phallic role demands impassivity; the prick obviously gets pleasure from his cruelty. The evidence of the pleasure undermines the rigid authority of the paternal position.

Lacan attributes Freud's success with his hysterics to the attentive court Freud paid them.[3] Another contributor to *L'Arc* 58, Luce Irigaray, takes up Lacan's suggestion in her reading of Freud where she writes: 'It would be too risky, it seems, to admit that the father could be a seducer, and even eventually that he desires to have a daughter in order to seduce her. That he wishes to become an analyst in order to exercise—by means of hypnosis, suggestion, transference, interpretation bearing upon the sexual economy, upon proscribed sexual representations—a lasting seduction upon the hysteric.'[4] Irigaray suggests that the risk ('it would be too risky') is avoided by 'this cloak of the law with which he covers his desire, and his sex organ [*son sexe*]' (*Speculum*, p. 42). In the place of Father Freud's prick, we have his phallocentrism: the normative law that denies the desire it cloaks (protects and covers).

Irigaray's reading of Freud would uncloak that desire. Her rape of the Father (as aggressive and admiring as any rape) is thoroughly Lacanian. The inquiry into Freud's phallocentric cloak reveals Lacan's prick. As the rallying of women around Lacan in *L'Arc* suggests, he gets all the girls because, tantalizingly, he unveils his desire, manages to show his prick, to let the girls know that he wants them.

Irigaray never mentions Lacan's name in her book *Speculum*. Nor in her contribution to *L'Arc* 58. Not that she is simply avoiding a confrontation with this powerful influence. 'La "Mécanique" des fluides' (*L'Arc*, 58, pp. 49–55) is certainly an article 'on Lacan', in its own fashion. Lacan is quoted (his name does appear in the footnotes, just not in the text). Not that out of some principle of discretion she never mentions the name of the object of her attentions. Freud's name appears throughout 'La Tache aveugle d'un vieux rêve de symétrie', her reading of Freud in *Speculum*.

In Lacan's writing, the Name-of-the-Father is the Law. The legal assignation of a Father's Name to a child is meant to call a halt to uncertainty about the identity of the father. If the mother's femininity (both her sexuality and her untrustworthiness) were affirmed, the Name-of-the-Father would always be in doubt, always be subject to the question of the mother's morality. Thus the Name-of-the-Father must be arbitrarily and absolutely imposed, thereby instituting the reign of patriarchal law. However, the father's penis is reminiscent of the extra-legal beginnings of the child. The Father's Name is, by law, unique; the father's penis is but one of many organs involved in the production of the child. If the Name-of-the-Father is phallocentric law, then the father's prick is the derision of his Name.

Refusing Lacan's Name is to refuse to read Lacan as Lawgiver and rather to choose to read his text as body, as that which is not sublimated nor unified but which is open to intercourse. Irigaray weaves a sinuous text, artfully combining Lacanian threads with remarks against or beyond Lacan. Above all, there is a tremendous fluidity since Lacan's threads are not consistently identified or set off from 'her own'. She plunges into this sensuous swim at a point indicated by Lacan: 'What is in excess in relation to form— such as the feminine sex (organ) [*le sexe féminin*]—being necessarily rejected as beneath or beyond the system presently in effect. "Woman does not exist." As regards discursivity' ('Mécanique', *L'Arc*, 58, p. 51). In both *Encore* and *Télévision*[5] Lacan repeatedly asserts that 'woman does not exist'. Discursivity, the reigning system, cannot include woman, because it demands the solid, the identical to the exclusion of the fluid. 'Nonetheless the woman creature, it speaks. ... It speaks "fluid"' ('Mécanique', p. 51). Hysterical speech, formless and useless like the discharges of a womb. Like Lacan who babbles on for years before anyone understands him?

'La "Mécanique" des fluides' is 'about' the hegemony of solids in physics and metaphysics with its concurrent exclusion and attempted recuperations of fluids and their peculiar qualities. The characteristics of solids are solidary with phallocentric rigidity as well as the metaphysical privileging of identity. And psychoanalysis is implicated in this 'solidarity'. 'Thus, if any psychic economy is organized in terms of the phallus (or Phallus), one could wonder what this pre-eminence owes to a teleology of reabsorption of the fluid into a solid [consistent] form' ('Mécanique', p. 51).

But Irigaray is not content merely to designate the fluid as that which leaks out of solid discursivity. She drifts away from Lacan (in this protean text the notion of rupture is nonsense) inasmuch as she would not only designate the fluid as simply other, 'beneath or beyond the system', but would study it as having a mechanics of its own. It is the specific characteristics of fluids that are ignored by the 'long-standing complicity between rationality and a mechanics restricted to solids' ('Mécanique', p. 49). So woman speaks but cannot be heard. 'Yet one must know how to listen otherwise than in good form(s) in order to hear what it [woman] says. That it's continuous...compressible, dilatable, viscous, conductible, diffusible...that it allows itself to be easily traversed by flows on account of its conductibility...; that it mixes with bodies in a like state, dilutes itself at times in a nearly homogeneous fashion, which renders problematic the distinction between the one and the other; and besides, that it is already diffuse "in itself", which disconcerts any attempt at static identification"' ('Mécanique', p. 52).

In an instant of distinction Irigaray would impute that Lacan, despite his allusive mobility, invests the details, the mechanics, with a protective rigidity. The mechanics in question in Lacanian physics are those of the object *a*. The object is designated by a lower case 'a' to place it in a relation of inferiority to the capital A in Lacan's writing which stands for the *Autre*, the radical Other that is other than any objectifiable other. The object *a* is a domestication of the Other. The relation to the Other fails, whereas the relation to the object works; so the object *a* allows for a mechanics that describes its workings.

The object *a* 'sets itself in the place of that of the Other which cannot be glimpsed' (*Encore*, p. 58). The structure is analogous to Freud's mechanics of the fetish object.[6] For Freud the fetish object appears in the place of the Mother's absent phallus ('the attribute of the Other which cannot be glimpsed'). Lacan goes on to say that the object *a* 'somewhere fills...the role of that which comes in (the) place of the missing partner' (ibid.). In the place of Woman (who does not exist: 'It's true, like it or not, if the sexual relation does not exist, there are no ladies', *Encore*, p. 54) is the object *a*.

Phallic sexuality is the relation to this object which obstructs and replaces the relation to the Other (to Woman). The effect of the phallic order is that phallic pleasure cannot but doom to failure any sexual relation (relation between the sexes). The man's dealings are with the object *a*.

Now, according to Irigaray, the object *a* usually refers back to a fluid state. 'Milk, luminous flow, acoustic waves,...not to mention the gases that are inhaled, emitted, differently perfumed, urine, saliva, blood, plasma itself, etc. But, such are not the *a*'s enumerated in the theory' ('Mécanique', p. 53). The object *a* of the theory (Lacan's, to be sure) finds its paradigm in the faeces. The faecal flow is interrupted by contraction of the sphincter, and a turd—solid, distinct, countable—is created. 'Could the very object of desire, including that of psychoanalysts, be the transformation of fluid into solid?' (ibid.). She asks why sperm never functions as an '*a*'. Whereas the problem of castration is posed by psychoanalysis, the problem of fluid-sperm as 'an obstacle to the generalization of an economy restricted to solids' (ibid.) is never taken up. Her momentary conclusion (the plasticity of this article must not be forgotten) is that 'the misappreciation [*méconnaissance*] of a specific economy of fluids...is perpetuated by psychoanalytic science' (ibid.). The real risk is not castration, but an instability in which any break is out of the question.

Of course, that is hardly a break with Lacan. Lacan has it that the phallic order short-circuits fluid desire by fixing it onto an object. The sexual relation falls short and the human being reproduces itself, produces an object distinguished from the flow. '[The speaking body] only reproduces itself thanks to a miscarriage of what it means to say, since what it means to say...is its actual pleasure [*jouissance effective*]. And it is by failing to obtain that pleasure that it reproduces itself—which is to say, by fucking' (*Encore*, p. 109).

Irigaray churns up the current in Lacan that is always threatening to overturn the 'phallocentric system'. She joins Lacan the ladies' man, even Lacan the prick—for both are equally seductive and disruptive—in an attempt to drown Lacan The Man who clings precariously to the solid system.

In 1974, the year of *L'Arc* 58, Lacan starred in a strange and frustrating television programme. The format pretended to be an interview, but Lacan arrogantly eluded the very questions he himself had commanded. Not that there was no correspondence between question and answer, but Lacan coquettishly avoided any man-to-man confrontation. As the programme opens, Lacan begins: 'I always speak the truth: not the whole truth [*pas toute*], because one does not succeed at speaking the whole truth' (*Télé-vision*, p. 9). This beginning bespeaks an outrageous imperious-ness. Yet this performance is the ultimate in femininity. '[Woman] lends herself readily to the perversion which I hold to be The Man's. Which leads her to the well-known masquerade, which is not the lie which ingrates—solidary with The Man—charge her with. Rather the on-the-off-chance of being prepared so that The Man's fantasy can find its hour of truth in her. This is not excessive since truth is already a woman by not being the whole truth [*de n'être pas toute*], not wholly to be said [*pas toute à se dire*] in any case' (*Télévision*, p. 64).

The 'hour of truth' is possible. It is only the attempt to erect a systematic ontology, fixing that truth, which is scandalized by the 'lie' of truth's instability. 'The fluid...is, by nature, unstable. ...Woman never speaks *pareil* [similar, like, equal]. What she emits is flowing [*fluent*], fluctuating. Cheating [*Flouant*]' ('Mé-canique', p. 52). That which flows and fluctuates is suspect and shady in the view of those 'solidary with The Man'. The fluid is *flouant*. The masquerade which gives the truth is hated as a lie.

The question 'Lacan and Women?' finds its evanescent 'hour of truth' in the unsettling encounter, in which desire pointedly invades the arena of intellect, between The Man and his stable of floozies, between these principled women and that shameless floozie Lacan.

4 *Encore* Encore

The questions of the last chapter must be asked and re-asked. *Encore* poses a serious puzzle: what does it mean that Lacan should give a seminar saying 'Woman does not exist' at the moment when the impact of feminism is peaking and in full cognizance of that feminism? Once again I would like to investigate *Encore*, but this time, so as to produce a different reading–one that does not simply find what it expects but rather can be surprised–I will alter my context by taking as my companion Stephen Heath's article 'Difference',[1] an English reading that criticizes *Encore* from a feminist perspective.

Heath begins by informing us that '*Encore*, Lacan's 1972/73 seminar [is] devoted to "what Freud expressly left aside, the *Was will das Weib*? the *What does woman want?*"' Heath situates Lacan's relation to the woman question in a devotion–'seminar *devoted* to "what Freud . . . left aside"'–a devotion, a fidelity, a constancy. Yet Lacan said nothing of devotion; he used the word 'aborder' (come to, enter upon, approach, accost): 'What I *aborde* [accost] this year is what Freud expressly left aside, the *Was will das Weib?*'[2] Lacan speaks of a beginning (from 'aborder' –'d'abord', first, in the beginning), a beginning of a relation to this question; far from devoting himself to woman he is simply at the stage of approach, first and rather aggressive encounter.

The woman's choice appears obvious: what does she want? devotion or to be accosted. Freud expressly left her aside (*à côté*, in Lacan's words). Oddly, 'accost' comes precisely from 'à côté'– you come up alongside someone, you approach from the side and speak: 'Wanna go for a ride?' 'Wanna see my etchings?'–'What does Woman want?'

(Lacan tells of a recent trip to Milan, and an ambiguous encounter with a lady from the Italian Women's Liberation Movement. In Lacan's words: 'She was *really* [and then a coy ellipsis in the place of the adjective] I told her–*Come tomorrow morning, I'll explain to you what it's all about.*' There is no further mention of the encounter with the Italian lady, simply the approach and the line–'Come tomorrow morning, I'll explain to you what it's all about.' And then Lacan continues: 'This *affair* of sexual relations [does 'this' refer backwards to the Italian lady, or forwards–a sexy moment of ambiguity?], this business of sexual relations if there is a point from which it might become clear [the ambiguity continues, the affair with the Italian lady precisely needs clarification], if there is a point from which it might become clear it's precisely from the side of the ladies [*du côté des dames*, from the ladies' side]'–p. 54.)

Freud left the side of the woman; Lacan has just arrived there; but Heath offers devotion, the man who will remain constantly at the woman's side. The choice is between Heath's gallant chivalry (he effacingly refers to himself as 'me not a woman'–p. 111; one of 'those not woman'–p. 99; he wrote this article to *honour a commitment* to some feminists–p. 111) and Lacan's cavalier approach ('Woman does not exist', '[women] don't know what they're saying, that's all the difference between them and me'–p. 68): chivalry or cavalier approach? The choice seems obvious, but is it?

Lacan in *Encore* speaks about chivalry in its historical form, courtly love. Lacan says that 'for the man, whose lady was entirely, in the most servile sense, his subject, [courtly love was] the only elegant way to pull out of the absence of any sexual relation' (p. 65). 'Courtly love', according to Lacan, 'is a totally refined way of supplementing the absence of sexual relations, by pretending that it is we who put the obstacle there' (ibid.). Courtly love obstructs the sight of the absence of a relation between the sexes. It appears, Lacan says, 'at the level of political degeneracy [when] it had to become evident that on the woman's side [*du côté de la femme*, from the woman's side, at the woman's side] there was something that could no longer work at all' (p. 79).

Chivalry then, devotion to the lady, is a way of supplementing, making up for, getting away from, masking the glaring absence ('it had to become evident') of sexual relations. This elegant code of devotion and fealty comes to fill in the gap so that the jam, the breakdown *du côté de la femme* will not be evident. At one point, Lacan compares Freud's discourse with courtly love. Freud leaves the woman's side; courtly love, chivalry pulls out so it need not see what goes on (or rather doesn't) at the woman's side. To choose chivalry (Heath's devotion) over macho aggression (Lacan's accosting the woman) is to choose to cover up a glaring absence, not the absence of a penis (Freud's castrated woman), not the woman's lack, but the lack of the woman to the man, the lack between them, lack of a 'between-them'.

But I haven't been fair with Heath. I've taken the word 'devoted' out of context; Lacan's seminar not Heath was devoted. I've left the context aside, left the side of the text. After a first approach, I've not been faithful to the text, not given a faithful representation.

Were I more faithful to context, were my paper more devoted to Heath, I would pick up the term 'suture', used without emphasis in this article, but the subject of an earlier Heath article on Lacan. Suture is a signal term at another intersection, the intersection of film theory and psychoanalysis. In the context of Lacanian film criticism, the context of the journal *Screen* (which is the context for Heath's reading of *Encore*), 'suture', like courtly love, is the supplementation of an absence, the joining of a gap by representation. In his 'Notes on Suture',[3] Heath notices a certain slide, a muddling slippage in the use of the term. You can look at *Screen*'s 'Dossier on Suture' for the details of this term's vicissitudes, but before I go too far afield out of devotion to Heath, let me simply say that for our purposes it is interesting to note two things: (1) this central term in Lacanian film theory is subject to a treacherous slide—that is, prone to infidelity of representation; and (2) this *Lacanian term* does not originate with Lacan, but at Lacan's side, with Jacques-Alain Miller, the editor of Lacan's seminars, and himself not a psychoanalyst.

Something about suture, this bastard Lacanian term, child of a lack of fidelity in representing the father, yet productive of a powerful transmission of Lacan into film theory...

Lacan talks about *glissement* (slippage, slide) along the signifying chain, from signifier to signifier. Theory is not metalinguistically immune to what Freud called displacement, which Lacan calls desire. In 'Notes on Suture', Heath remarks that Lacan displaces rather than assumes linguistics (p. 51). From different angles then, we keep rejoining unfaithful representation, slippery terms falling from their proper place, away from their authors, falling from authority, unauthorized.

Jacques-Alain Miller, who introduces the term suture in a presentation he gives at a Lacan seminar, begins his talk by questioning his own authority.[4] What right has he, not-a-psychoanalyst (we recall Heath's not-a-woman), by what is he authorized to talk? In the first sentence of Heath's article on *Encore*, after the quoted, doubly quoted (Lacan quoting Freud) 'What does Woman want?' appears a very long footnote about authorization. Like Miller, Heath begins his text with the question of the authority to speak of psychoanalysis. Heath, however, does not relate the question of authority to himself; he poses it as an assertion *about* psychoanalysis: 'psychoanalysis exists and is learned...in the analytic situation, cannot be contained, at best approached, in theoretical constructions...cannot be authorized by master or institution' (note, p. 52). Notice the word approached ('at best approached in theoretical constructions'). The 'approach' missing from the Lacan quote (Heath substitutes his own 'devoted') returns here in the footnote to that quote. Rather than containment, summation, possession, authorization, psychoanalysis is simply an approaching. *A border* not devotion; approaching not containment, not authorization.

Why does this footnote intercede (as if in reply) directly after the question 'What does Woman want?' To answer that question let us look at the part authorization plays in Heath's representation of feminism.

Interested in the relation of women to language, as a response to Lacan's statement that 'there is no woman but excluded by... the nature of words' (p. 68), Heath guides us on a brief tour through the major authors/authorities of French feminism, apologizing for the lack of detail in his summary panorama. In French feminism he finds statements about a feminine writing, writing which although not necessarily by a woman 'jams the machinery of theory' (this a quote from Luce Irigaray) or (this from Michèle Montrelay) 'ruins representation'. Heath parenthetically worries that Irigaray is 'close to Lacan' (perhaps right there at his side) and contrasts this French feminist writing with positions in American feminist sociolinguistics. The Americans want to '*reject*' the discursive specifications of woman as inconsistent, unfinished, fluid', want women—who have been segregated into a special 'women's language'—to accede to the use of 'neutral language' (p. 81). On the other hand, French feminists see 'neutral language' as itself an 'area of oppression, the alienation of difference in the order of the same of the phallus' and want to use the fluid, the inconsistent, the unfinished to undermine the oppressive 'phallic seriousness of meaning' (ibid.).

Across this encounter Heath seems to change positions, coming close to the position of Irigaray, herself close to Lacan.

In the French v. American feminist argument, Heath operates what in cinematic terms might be called a shot/reverse-shot. First shooting the French from the American view and then 'from the other side, as it were, reversing the perspective', he represents the oppressive assumptions of the American position as seen from the French perspective. His 'as it were', pointing with embarrassed pride to the forced analogy, the desired, too-desired analogy that goes coyly unnamed. 'Reversing the perspective', shot/reverse-shot, that is one of the cinematic specifications of the term 'suture' ('Notes on Suture', pp. 65–6). In 'Notes on Suture', Heath considers the restriction of suture to the shot/reverse-shot as an abuse of the term, a use we might call unauthorized. But here in the feminist argument, he evokes ('as it were') this bastard version of the already, originally illegitimate term 'suture'. And then as if in response to his own pleasure in the unauthorized suture, he winds up this section by endorsing for women a practice of language that goes against 'the orders of language', a practice of language that he calls *unauthorized* (p. 82).

What is this feminist practice of unauthorization? In *Encore*, Lacan defines an 'authorized thought', as 'a thought bequeathed with an author's name' (p. 51). Bequeathed, legally left: for example, from father to son. The authorized partakes of the legal and the name. The authorized, legitimate thought bears the author's name; the unauthorized, the illegitimate lacks the Name-of-the-Father. The Name-of-the-Father, let us here signal, is a powerful Lacanian term, actually a Lacanian displacement of what Freud bequeathed him/us, the Oedipal Father, absolute primal Father. Whereas Freud's Oedipal Father might be taken for a real, biological father, Lacan's Name-of-the-Father operates explicitly in the register of language. The Name-of-the-Father: the patronym, patriarchal law, patrilineal identity, language as our inscription into patriarchy. The Name-of-the-Father is the fact of the attribution of paternity by law, by language. Paternity cannot be perceived, proven, known with certainty; it must be instituted by judgement of the mother's word. Certainty in the supposition of one's biological father, one's 'real' father is always an imaginary effect (in Lacan's sense of the imaginary). The mother names the father (the paternity suit is an exposure of the law structuring the imaginary entity called a 'biological family';

the paternity suit: who ever heard of a maternity suit? a maternity dress, yet, but a maternity suit?). What guarantees the mother's word, the mother's fidelity to her word, in short, what guarantees the mother's fidelity? Any suspicion of the mother's infidelity betrays the Name-of-the-Father as the arbitrary imposition it is. The merest hint of the mother's infidelity threatens to expose what Lacan calls the symbolic (the register of the Name-of-the-Father), which is usually covered over, sutured, by the representations of what Lacan calls the imaginary, the imaginary of chivalry, the woman's presumed honour.

Infidelity then is a feminist practice of undermining the Name-of-the-Father. The unfaithful reading strays from the author, the authorized, produces that which does not hold as a reproduction, as a representation. Infidelity is *not* outside the system of marriage, the symbolic, patriarchy, but hollows it out, ruins it, from within. Unlike such infidelity, a new system, a feminist system, one constant, faithful to the tenets and dogmas of feminism would be but another Name-of-the-Father, feminism as a position and a possession.

By the end of his article, Heath is troubled by what he calls his 'confidence of knowledge, a certain position, a certain possession' (p. 111). About that 'confidence of knowledge', the difficulty of Heath's writing this article, the difficulty of feminist writing, one that is not a certainty of possession, author, authority, authorization. The 'confidence of knowledge' returns as his slip, his infidelity to his feminist commitment.

Perhaps the best characterization of a knowledge that isn't a possession is found in a parenthesis in Heath's first footnote, the one replying to 'What does Woman want?' the one about authorization. The parenthesis follows the statement that 'psychoanalysis cannot be authorized by master or institution' and reads: 'the analyst is not the possessor of a diploma but the site of a listening attention in which he or she is constantly surprised, reimplicated' (p. 52n). Possession of a diploma affords 'confidence of knowledge', but unauthorized science, feminist practice, affords the possibility of surprise. At the end of his article, Heath poses a working rule for such a practice of unauthorization: 'Alternative practices are alternative insofar as they transform the relations of the symbolic in representation. . . against the universalizing conditions of exchange: representation held to use' (p. 108). Surprise jams universalization, and a listening attention, an attentiveness to specification, guards against confidence, certainty of possession.

Alternative practice would refuse exchange value and produce only use value. Exchange value and use value: the context for these terms is Marx; the context of *Screen* is not only film, feminism and psychoanalysis; it is also, importantly, marxism, ideological criticism. *Encore* too makes explicit reference to Marx. Lacan states that his demonstration of use value is better than Marx's, since in Marx 'everything is summed up in exchange value' (p. 89). 'Everything' (the French word is 'tout') can recall the universalization (summing up) Heath says supports exchange value. *Tout*, the contained, the universalized, leads to exchange value, not use value. Lacan refers to woman as the *pas-tout* (not-everything), which term is a displacement not an assumption of Freud's notion of the woman as castrated, here, in Marxian terms, that which exceeds exchange value. Woman as the *pas-tout* (not-everything, not-all) is the refusal to sum up, to give a finished representation; the *pas-tout* is, in Heath's words, an alternative practice. In this context, it is important to notice what Heath ignores: that Lacan repeatedly specifies that any speaking being *regardless of sex* is free to place itself on either side, the side of *tout* (phallic universalization) or the side of the *pas-tout* (non-universalized, castrated, Freud would say).

On the side of the *pas-tout,* an alternative practice, outside exchange value: let us here think of Lévi-Strauss's exchange of women. The system of the Name-of-the-Father implies authorized possession of the woman, who since possessed can be exchanged. Infidelity is a use value, the use of the woman one does not possess, one is not authorized to exchange.

Lacan speaks of a knowledge that 'does not rest on exchange': a knowledge that is evaluated, valued, by its cost 'not as exchange, but as use', a very valuable knowledge because it is difficult 'less to acquire it than to enjoy it' (ibid.). The opposition exchange/use becomes, from one sentence to the next, the opposition acquire/enjoy, with the word for enjoy, 'jouir'. 'There, in the enjoying [*jouir,* use], the conquest of this knowledge is renewed each time it is exercised,' says Lacan, and we recall Heath's notion of psychoanalysis as a knowledge that is not contained, but rather affords constant surprises, constant reimplication. There is no 'confidence of knowledge' when it comes to using it, rather than exchanging it. It is the use, the enjoyment, the *jouissance,* which exceeds exchange. This opposition of *jouissance* and possession can refer to a legal meaning of *jouissance*, as having the use of something. Notice the example of usufruct, given in the dictionary under *jouissance*. 'Usufruct' is the right to the *jouissance* but *not the ownership* of something; in other words, you can use and enjoy it, but you cannot exchange it. 'The foundation of a knowledge', continues Lacan, 'is that the *jouissance* of exercising it is the same as that of acquiring it.' To enjoy, to use knowledge is always the surprise of the moment of acquisition, the approach.

The word 'jouissance' leads us back to the first page of Heath's reading of *Encore*, back to the first sentence which was interrupted by the long footnote on authorization. The sentence—not really a proper sentence at all—reads: 'From *Encore*, Lacan's 1972/73 seminar devoted to "what Freud expressly left aside, the *Was will das Weib?*, the *What does woman want?*" (Seminar xx, p. 75), [a superscripted '1' follows the page reference, leading to the long footnote on authorization, then after the '1' the text continues as follows:] this passage on female pleasure, enjoyment, *jouissance*.' What follows then is a long passage from *Encore*, but before we enter it, let us note that its subject is *jouissance*. Heath uses the French word and links it by apposition to female pleasure. If *jouissance* is a use value, which subverts exchange value, then it is a female pleasure, not restricted to biological females, but placing itself on the side of the *pas-tout*, the side of resistance to phallic universalization, the side of surprise.

The slated Lacan quote begins: 'just as with Saint Teresa—you only have to go and look at the Bernini statue in Rome to understand immediately that she's coming, no doubt about it'. Heath seizes immediately upon Lacan's certainty, Lacan's 'confidence of knowledge', emphasizing the 'you only have to go and look', and the 'no doubt about it'. Heath sees this as a low point in Lacan's discourse, a moment of appeal to a certainty in vision, and concludes that somewhere Lacan has a confidence about woman's mystery, woman's otherness. Heath finds here proof that beneath Lacan's fancy talk of signifiers lurks a sexist prejudice tied to an ideology of representation.

'No doubt, not the trace of any difficulty': in those words (p. 52) Heath condemns Lacan and yet this discussion of the Saint Teresa statue quotation concludes a page later in the following words: 'where a discourse appeals directly to an image, to an immediacy of seeing, as a point of its argument or demonstration, *one can be sure* that all difference is being elided, that the unity of some accepted vision is being reproduced' (p. 53, my italics). 'One can be sure': Heath's words reimplicate him in the 'confidence of knowledge' he is working to expose.

A listening attention to this Lacan quotation provides more surprise, more reimplication of Heath. 'She's coming, no doubt about it': 'coming' is Heath's translation of 'jouir', an important word in a quotation the reader has been prepared to centre on *jouissance*. 'Coming' is not noted as the translation of 'jouir', and is a surprisingly confident translation of a word which elsewhere (in his translator's introduction to Barthes's *Image—Music—Text*) Heath specifies as lacking a suitable English equivalent. Prefatory to the Barthes text, Heath confesses: 'I have no real answer to the problem [of translating 'jouir'] and have resorted to a series of words which in different contexts can contain at least some of that force.' And in the last sentence of the same Lacan quotation we are considering, Heath retains the French word *jouissance*, as a sign of its untranslatability, unrepresentability. It appears that the word 'jouissance' itself can refuse exchange value, and be limited to use value. But in the first sentence of the long Lacan quotation, Heath writes 'she's coming, no doubt about it'; here, Heath can translate 'without the trace of a difficulty'. Here he can translate, can exchange, can represent 'jouir' feeling ('as it were') 'no doubt about it'.

'No doubt about it, not the trace of a difficulty', Heath complains of Lacan's vision of Teresa's *jouissance*. Yet Heath's own lack of doubt is precisely his difficulty, what at the end of the article he will term 'the difficulty of writing, of my return in discourse as a certain possession'. The difficulty of a *jouissance* that isn't a possession, Lacan's knowledge that is difficult 'not to acquire but to enjoy' is, we said before, the difficulty of feminist writing, the difficulty of keeping infidelity from becoming fidelity to a system of infidelity.

Heath says: 'difficult for me, for me not a woman' (p. 111). This 'not a woman' should be related to Lacan's *pas-tout*, the feminine side as that which is not universalized, not faithful, not constant to an identity. Heath writes as not-a-woman, thus writing from the feminine, unauthorized position, but his difficulty is a return of a phallic representation of self; not-a-woman becomes summed-up as 'a man'.

Lacan in the Saint Teresa quotation classes his own *Écrits* with the mystics, that is, on the side of female *jouissance*, the side of *pas-tout*. And like Heath writing as not-a-woman, Lacan too finds a difficulty. Let us grant a listening attention to the following paragraph from *Encore*: 'There is the male manner of revolving around [the fact of an absence of any sexual relation], there is the male manner and then the other, which I don't designate in an*other* way because it is *that* which, this year, I am in the process of elaborating–how, in the female manner, *that* is elaborated' (pp. 53–4). Note the repetition of the verb elaborate which approaches *his* elaboration to the female manner of elaboration. Note also the use of the phrase 'in the female manner', an immediate and blatant infidelity to his own specification that he will *not* designate the non-male in any other way than as 'the other manner'. But, also, 'designation' cannot be in an*other* way, since as designation it is always in the male manner, hence 'I will not designate in an *other* way'. The word 'that' is my translation of *ça*, also the usual French for the *id*. So that the phrase which I rendered as 'how, in the female manner, *that* is elaborated' should also be translated as 'how, in the female manner, the id elaborates itself'.

Lacan continues: '*That* is elaborated from the *pas-tout*. Only, since until now *that* has not been explored much, the *pas-tout*, *that* evidently gives me a bit of difficulty.' 'A bit of difficulty' is my translation of Lacan's 'un peu de mal'. His attempt to elaborate in the manner of the *pas-tout*, like Heath's, gives him 'a bit of difficulty'. But a close homonym for 'mal' is the word meaning male, a word already pronounced at the beginning of this paragraph in the phrase 'there is the male manner of revolving around': 'the male manner', *la façon mâle*. So in a paragraph hardly immune to the insistence of word-play, in 'a bit of difficulty', 'un peu de mal', one finds also 'a bit of maleness'. Lacan is *pas-tout* in the female manner: that is (*pas-tout* taken adverbially), Lacan is not completely in the female manner; there remains a bit of maleness. Lacan's elaboration is not completely faithful to the other manner.

Heath's text itself yields an implicit link between the bits of difficult/bits of maleness of these two not-women (Lacan and Heath). At the end of his paper Heath admits that his 'confidence of knowledge' is probably 'an appropriation of [feminism], another strategem of oppression'. Then he continues: 'for instance, a little example', and gives an example from this very paper of a certain patronizing tone that returns in his praise of a woman film-maker. Heath's introductory phrase 'a little example' recalls an earlier moment when he writes 'an example *fairly small*, but significant' (my italics) (p. 66). The 'little example' at the end of the article is Heath's own 'bit of difficulty, bit of maleness'; the earlier 'fairly small example' is not Heath's difficulty, but something from Lacan. Implicitly through the echo between 'fairly small example' and 'little example', Heath's text ties together Lacan's and his own infidelity, but the two are never linked explicitly.

Here then is the 'fairly small, but significant' piece of evidence against Lacan: Lacan speculates, says Heath, that 'it is through sexual reality that the signifier came into the world' (p. 66). Heath has specified that this statement, which might imply a recourse to some reality that grounds signification, is merely speculative, but he goes on to elaborate the consequence 'if that speculation is accepted'. It isn't certain, even to Heath, that Lacan ever accepts that speculation, but Heath none the less refers back to the sentence throughout the rest of the article as if it were certain.

Heath worries that 'Lacan is close to Freud's laying down of arms before the ultimate reality of the great enigma of the biological fact of the duality of the sexes'. Lacan is troublingly 'close to Freud', just as later Irigaray will be dangerously 'close to Lacan'. The danger is that biology as origin of the subject will exclude history as production of the subject. Heath concludes: 'to say that it is through sexual reality that the signifier comes into the world is *not far* from deriving the phallus as privileged signifier from an *essence* in nature' (my italics). Heath fears Lacan is approaching ('not far') essences, and what is more dangerous to political transformation than an ideology of essence?

But essence makes a very surprising come-back in Heath's paper by way of the problematic feminist film *Riddles of the Sphinx*. That film by Laura Mulvey and Peter Wollen is close to Irigaray who is close to Lacan who is close to Freud. And all these proximities relate to another set of commonplace proximities, the nearness of woman to inconsistency, narcissism, otherness, God, truth and the unconscious. *Riddles of the Sphinx*, Irigaray, other French feminists, by positing a closeness between woman and unconscious, by advocating a feminine practice of writing, 'feminine' rather than 'neutral language', are in danger. According to Heath, 'the danger in all this is it matches perfectly with the historical positions of patriarchal society in which "woman" has been constantly identified as a locus of dis-order' (p. 73). The difference between Lacan, the French, *Riddles of the Sphinx*, on the one hand, and 'the positions of patriarchal society' on the other, hinges on Heath's word 'identified'. Lacan does not identify 'woman'; thus does not universalize, possess, restrict her. He is explicitly *not* dealing with an identity of woman; rather he is dealing with the impossibility of a female identity, since identity passes through the Name-of-the-Father. Lacan bars through the definite article 'La' of 'La femme'; and that bar makes the general term 'woman', as opposed to the singular 'a woman', impossible to say in French. It is not that woman is identified on the side of the *pas-tout*, rather she is not completely (*pas-tout*) identified or identifiable.

Lacan's word-play suggests that the id is elaborated in the female manner. Heath declares that 'the equation of woman and unconscious leads only to essence' (p. 74). A pun is not an equation, but not exactly innocent either. However, 'the equation of woman and unconscious' is suggested not just by Lacan or even Irigaray, but also by *Riddles of the Sphinx*. And Heath cannot disregard the feminism of that film. So near the end of his paper, Heath comes to say, 'As in *Riddles of the Sphinx*, the risk of essence may have to be taken.'

Lacan cavalierly takes that risk. In *Encore* he says: '*La femme* [Woman] cannot be written except by barring *La*. There is no *La femme* [there is no universalized woman] since—I have already risked the term, and why should I give it a second glance?—in essence she is not complete [*pas-toute*, she is not every woman, she is not completely in her essence]' (p. 68). 'I have risked the term essence', Lacan says. 'I have already risked the term': a return to Lacan's earlier risking of the term brings us to an interesting strategy for alternative practice. 'You will notice', Lacan says on the occasion of his first use of the term, 'that I spoke of essence, just like Aristotle. . . . That means that these old words are completely utilizable' (p. 55). He goes on to promote a utilitarianism which is not a recourse to the utilitarian (after all he said utilizable, not useful), but a necessary analysis of what 'these old words. . . are used for'. We are not far from ideological criticism.

'Essence', that old word, must be hollowed out, reinscribed as a use value, unauthorized, detached from the privilege of Aristotle as author's name. An alternative practice may have to use old words: 'infidelity', for example, not very appropriate to feminist discussions of alternatives to bourgeois marriage.

Heath quotes Freud saying, 'we *make use* of what is obviously an inadequate empirical and conventional equation'[5] (my italics) of active and male, passive and female. Lacan is close to Freud's 'making use', but he pushes a little harder. 'One must make use, but really use them up, really wear out these old words, wear them threadbare, use them until they're thoroughly hackneyed' (p. 56). What a way of ruining exchange value by use!

Perhaps this explains the annoying and embarrassing insistence of 'phallus' and 'castration' in Lacan. Maybe he's using them up, running the risk of essence, running dangerously close to patri-archal positions, so as to wear 'phallus' and 'castration' out, until they're thoroughly hackneyed. But probably not completely, *pas-tout*. In every alternative practice, every elaboration in the other manner, including the present one, the one you are reading, *un peu de mal*, a bit of difficulty, a bit of maleness, returns.

It is this infidelity that, fortunately, ruins the complete authorization of feminism.

5 The Father's Seduction

The first third of Luce Irigaray's *Speculum de l'autre femme* is called 'The Blind Spot of an Old Dream of Symmetry'. It is a close reading of 'Femininity', one of Freud's *New Introductory Lectures on Psycho-Analysis* (1933). This encounter between Irigaray's feminist critique and Freud's final text on woman is an important training ground for a new kind of battle, a feminine seduction/disarming/unsettling of the positions of phallocratic ideology. Irigaray's tactic is a kind of reading: close reading, which separates the text into fragments of varying size, quotes it and then comments with various questions and associations. She never sums up the meaning of Freud's text, nor binds all her commentaries, questions, associations into a unified representation, a coherent interpretation. Her commentaries are full of loose ends and unanswered questions. As a result, the reader does not so easily lose sight of the incoherency and inconsistency of the text.

That could be seen as a victory for feminism. The Man's order is disturbed by the woman with the impertinent questions and the incisive comments. But as with all seductions, the question of complicity poses itself. The dichotomy active/passive is always equivocal in seduction, that is what distinguishes it from rape. So Freud might have been encouraging Irigaray all along, 'asking for it'. 'By exhibiting this "symptom", this crisis-point in metaphysics where the sexual "indifference" which assured metaphysics its coherence and "closure" finally exposes itself, Freud proposes it to analysis: his text asking to be heard, to be read' (*Speculum*, p. 29).

Freud might have seduced Irigaray. It might be psychoanalysis that has won over feminism. The very strategy of reading with which Irigaray works Freud over is presented by Freud himself earlier in these *New Introductory Lectures* where he writes, 'we ask the dreamer, too, to free himself from the impression of the manifest dream, to divert his attention from the dream as a whole on to the separate portions of its content and to report to us in succession everything that occurs to him in relation to each of these portions—what associations present themselves to him if he focuses on each of them separately.'[1]

Freud's text asks for analysis. Not just any analysis, but the peculiar technique developed in psychoanalysis for dealing with dreams and other 'symptoms'. Freud proposed the model of the rebus for understanding dreams. According to the dictionary, a rebus is 'a riddle composed of words or syllables depicted by symbols or pictures that suggest the sound of the words or syllables they represent'. As a total picture, a unified representation, the rebus makes no sense. It is only by separating the picture into its elements, dealing with them one at a time, making all possible associations, that one can get anywhere. So psychoanalysis in its technique if not its theory offers an alternative to coherent, unified representation.

The rebus-text shatters the manifest unity so as to produce a wealth of associations which must necessarily be reduced if the goal of interpretation is to reach a final, definitive meaning, the 'latent dream-thoughts'. The unconscious is reappropriated to the model of consciousness—a circumscription analogous to the reappropriation of otherness, femininity to sameness, masculinity. Whereas Freud proposes the rebus as merely a path to the 'latent thoughts', Irigaray radicalizes Freud's rebus. Irigaray's dream-analysis ('The Blind Spot of an Old *Dream* of Symmetry') does not offer a final latent thought, but merely presents the abundance of associations, not editing those that 'lead nowhere'.

Yet Irigaray's encounter with Freud is not a psychoanalysis. Freud is not there to associate. Irigaray both asks questions (the analyst's role) and supplies associations (the dreamer's role). And since many questions go unanswered they appear directed to the reader, who thus becomes the dreamer. She does not aim to decipher Freud's peculiar psyche, but rather to unravel 'an old dream', everyone's dream, even Irigaray's dream. The dream is everyone's inasmuch as everyone is within 'the metaphysical closure', inasmuch as any reader is a 'subject', which is to say has been philosophically reduced to a unified, stable, sexually indifferent subject, trapped in the old dream of symmetry.

('Symmetry' from the Greek *summetros*—'of like measure'; from *sun*—'like, same', and *metron*—measure'. Symmetry is appropriating two things to like measure, measure by the same standard: for example the feminine judged by masculine standards. Judged by masculine measures, woman is inadequate, castrated.)

On the first page of *Speculum*, Irigaray interrupts Freud's text with the attributive indicator: 'he says, they [masculine plural] say'. She repeatedly does that, attributing Freud's words to both a masculine singular and a masculine plural subject pronoun. The old dream belongs to any subject, to anyone speaking and therefore in the position of subject. 'Every theory of the "subject" [Every theory about the subject as well as every theory produced by a subject] will always have been appropriate(d) to the "masculine"' (*Speculum*, p. 165). The neutral 'subject' is actually a desexualized, sublimated guise for the masculine sexed being. Woman can be subject by fitting male standards which are not appropriate to, cannot measure any specificity of femininity, any difference. Sexual indifference is not lack of sexuality, but lack of any different sexuality, the old dream of symmetry, the other, woman, circumscribed into woman as man's complementary other, his appropriate opposite sex.

But what of '*the blind spot* of an old dream of symmetry'? What is the blind spot? What cannot be seen, what is excluded from the light? According to Freud, the sight of woman's genitalia horrifies the young boy because he sees an absence. Mark that he does not see what is there, he sees the absence of a phallus. Nothing to see, nothing that looks like a phallus, nothing of like measure (*summetros*), no coherent visual representation in a familiar form. Nothing to see becomes nothing of worth. The privilege of sight over other senses, oculocentrism, supports and unifies phallocentric, sexual theory (theory—from the Greek *theoria*, from *theoros*, 'spectator', from *thea*, 'a viewing'). *Speculum* (from *specere*, 'to look at') makes repeated reference to the oculocentrism of theory. 'Every theory of the "subject" will always have been appropriate(d) to the "masculine"'. Every *theoria*, every viewing of the subject will have always been according to phallomorphic standards. Hence there is no valid representation of woman, but only a lack.

The female sex organs are the blind spot. Freud's theory must occult female sexuality, in order to manifest symmetry. But a blind spot can also be thought as the locus of greatest resistance in a dream, the least easily interpretable point and thus the most tantalizing. To call a text a dream in a Freudian context is not like calling it an illusion. To point to the blind spot of a dream is

not a moral condemnation. For it to be a moral condemnation, it
would be grounded in an ethic of absolute *luc*idity and en*light*en-
ment. The etymology of such words implies the morality of oculocentrism. Dreams are the 'royal road to the unconscious' and ask
for reading destructive of unified 'phallomorphic' representation,
the very reading Irigaray gives. The locus of greatest resistance,
'the blind spot' is the heart of the dream, the crisis-point crying,
begging for analysis.

Blind also like Oedipus is blinded. Freud is assimilated by
Irigaray to Oedipus. Freud, man, is never really out of the
Oedipus complex, never resolves his Oedipal phase. According to
Freud, the end of the Oedipus complex marks the end of the boy's
phallic phase. The phallic phase is characterized by the opposition phallic/castrated. In that phase there is no representation of
an other sex–the vagina, for example, is 'unknown'. Supposedly,
the difference between the phallic phase and adult sexuality is
that the dichotomy phallic/castrated gives way to the opposition
masculine/feminine. But if, as Irigaray finds in her reading of
Freud, the boy, the man, never resolves his Oedipal complex,
then he never leaves the phallic phase, and the opposition mascu-
line/feminine merely masks the opposition phallic/castrated. 'A
boy's mother is the first object of his love, and she remains so too
during the formation of his Oedipus complex and, *in essence, all
through his life*' (*NIL*, p. 118, my italics). Woman's destiny is to
become her husband's mother: 'A marriage is not made secure
until the wife has succeeded in making her husband her child as
well and in acting as a mother to him' (*NIL*, pp. 133–4). The
blind spot is the price of man's inability to escape his Oedipal destiny. Theory cannot see woman, but can only represent, re-pre-
sent, make present again endlessly, 'all through his life', Mother,
the masculine subject's *own* original complementary other.

Oedipus/Freud is an old riddle-solver. Oedipus solved the
riddle of the sphinx; Freud learned to read the rebus of dreams.
In the Freud text that Irigaray analyzes there is another riddle at
stake: 'Throughout history people have knocked their heads
against the riddle of the nature of femininity.' Yet Irigaray never
quotes or comments on this sentence. It occurs on the second
page of 'Femininity' and is followed by four lines of poetry–the
only poetry in this text. Irigaray only begins her reading of 'Femininity' after the poetry, in fact immediately after the poetry,
thus ignoring the first two pages of text. Reading *Speculum*, one

would never notice she does not begin at the beginning, for the paragraph she does start with 'makes sense' as an opening for Freud's lecture.

What are we to make of this exclusion of a large section of the text? Although here and there a few words or even a short sentence are omitted from Irigaray's reinscription of Freud, this is the only exclusion of such major proportion. Perhaps we must read this as another blind spot of an old dream of symmetry.

The section omitted is introductory and diverse, speaking of many things and not just on the topic of femininity. So one of the effects of Irigaray's omission is to give a more consistent, more unified representation of the text. In the same way, omitting the poetry homogenizes the discourse. The heterogeneous must be ignored by phallocentrism. Irigaray's forgetting renders Freud's text more phallocentric. Perhaps, then, the 'forgetting' is a tactical decision. Does she choose to ignore the materiality of the text in order to delineate and condemn the 'phallocentric theory'? She does not consistently use this tactic. At other moments in *Speculum* she emphasizes the crisis-points of confusion and contradiction, signalling the workings of the unconscious and the 'feminine' in Freud's text. Is it the inconsistency of her strategy, the lack of unity to her reading, that makes it most effective as an unsettling of phallocentric discourse?

Whatever the foundation for it, her omission, like Freud's 'blind spot', has the effect of begging for analysis, implicating her reader in the kind of reading she is doing. In this addendum to Irigaray's dream-work, this investigation of her 'blind spot', I would like to spend some time on the lines of poetry, as the least homogenized part of Freud's discourse, most resistant to an economy of the same. In this I am following the lead of another feminist, Lacanian reader, Shoshana Felman, who has written: '*Literature . . . is the unconscious of psychoanalysis*; . . . the unthought out shadow in psychoanalytic *theory* is precisely its own involvement with literature; . . . literature *in* psychoanalysis functions precisely as its "*unthought*": as the condition of possibility *and* the self-subversive *blind spot* of psychoanalytic *thought*.'[2] Felman's terms are resonant with those at play in Irigaray. The 'shadow in *theory*' calls to the oculocentric etymology of theory, and the appearance of the 'blind spot', also in that visual register, implicates this quotation in our present investigation. 'Literature' in Felman's discussion plays the same role (support and blind spot) in relation to psychoanalytic theory as 'the feminine' in

Irigaray's reading. It might be appropriate to look at the effect of this poetry on Freud's 'Femininity'.

Freud has just said: 'Throughout history people have knocked their heads against the riddle of the nature of femininity' and then he quotes: 'Heads in hieroglyphic bonnets/Heads in turbans and black birettas/Heads in wigs and thousand other/Wretched, sweating heads of humans.' A puzzling inclusion, in many ways. Why quote poetry about heads instead of about woman? The poem has the effect of emphasizing the marginal word 'heads', which is used in Freud's sentence in a figurative sense and ought to efface itself. Yet the poetry, repeating the word four times, makes 'heads' the dominant word in the sentence. The 'riddle of femininity' is eclipsed by an obsession with heads.

Irigaray suggests (*Speculum*, p. 39) that in Freud's theory the materiality of sex is obliterated by 'the Idea of sex' (she capitalizes to recall Plato and metaphysics). In other words, the riddle of sex, of sexual difference, the puzzling otherness there in its unresolved materiality is occulted, leaving in its place metaphysics, the Idea, in other words, 'heads...heads...heads'.

The enigmatic 'hieroglyphic bonnet' suggests Egypt and in this riddle context reminds us of the riddle of the Sphinx. We think of Oedipus and the way solving riddles leads to blindness. A 'solved' riddle is the reduction of heterogeneous material to logic, to the homogeneity of logical thought, which produces a blind spot, the inability to see the otherness that gets lost in the reduction. Only the unsolved riddle, the process of riddle-work before its final completion, is a confrontation with otherness.

Hieroglyphs themselves are a sort of riddle. Indeed, like a rebus, they present pictures which as a whole are not unified, and can only be read if one distinguishes the elements. 'Hieroglyphic' has the figurative sense of 'having a hidden meaning' and also 'hard to read, undecipherable'. As if the mysterious 'hieroglyphic bonnet' were itself a hieroglyph, this reader cannot determine if it is undecipherable or has a hidden meaning she cannot uncover. Such is also the puzzle of this entire poetic interruption. Why did Freud put it here? Why did Irigaray forget it?

The four lines are from Heinrich Heine's *Nordsee* (The Baltic), from a section of the poem entitled 'Fragen' (Questions). As an intrusion into Freud's lecture the poem indeed poses many questions: Why a poem about heads? Why a poem here and nowhere else? What is a hieroglyphic bonnet? Perhaps this hieroglyphic intrusion is not unlike Irigaray's interruptions. She often inserts a parenthetic question mark into Freud's or her own text, not altering the statement, but merely calling it into question. Much of her commentary consists in merely asking questions. And the largest section of her next book *Ce Sexe qui n'en est pas un* is, like Heine's poem, entitled 'Questions'.[3] Of course, unlike Irigaray's questions, Heine's are well buried. Freud's text only attributes the lines to *Nordsee*, not mentioning the title 'Fragen'. (Although it appears in a footnote to the English translation, the title 'Fragen' is in neither the German nor the French versions.) And there are no questions in the four lines of poetry quoted. Simply the reader's question: Why are these lines here?

None the less, might not Irigaray's impertinent questions already be implicit in the disruption to Freud's lecture, the interruption of his discourse, the distraction from his main point, wrought by Heine's poetry, Heine's 'Fragen'? After all, it can be construed to make her point about the sublimation of sex into 'heads'. Does she forget the poem so as to forget her already inscribed place in Freud's text? her own complicity in the dream symmetry she decries? Is she not reducing Freud to a single discourse, thus making his text more phallic, more centred? Perhaps any text can be read as either body (site of contradictory drives and heterogeneous matter) or Law? The exclusion of the Heine poem serves to place Freud more firmly on the side of the Law, which enables Irigaray to be more firm, more certain of her position against him. To be against the Law is to be outside the Law. But to be against a body is a more ambiguous, unsettling position.

In Heine's 'Questions' a youth asks the sea to answer 'life's hidden riddle, the riddle primeval and painful'. He asks specifically: 'Tell me, what signifies man? From whence doth he come? And where doth he go?' There is no answer, only the murmuring of the sea. The poem then ends with the line: 'And a fool is awaiting the answer.'[4]

At the beginning of the section called 'Questions' in *Ce Sexe*, Irigaray writes: 'Since the writing and publication of *Speculum*, many questions have been asked. And this book is, in a way, a collection of questions. It does not "really" answer them. It pursues their questioning. It continues to interrogate' (p. 119). The fool waits for an answer. Irigaray is not interested in the answer. She pursues a ceaseless questioning which has not time and is not foolish enough to wait for an answer.

The first part of Irigaray's 'Questions' takes place in a philosophy seminar, where, in response to *Speculum,* she has been invited as 'authority on women', for the students to ask her questions. The situation is somewhat analogous to that of 'Femininity', in which Freud is lecturing on women, professing about women, allowing the audience to learn from his expertise. Tied up in this dialectic of questions and answers is the problematic of 'authority on women'. To have a theory of woman is already to reduce the plurality of woman to the coherent and thus phallocentric representations of theory. Irigaray, as professor of woman, is in the role of 'subject of theory', subject theorizing, a role appropriate to the masculine. She is in Freud's role, dreaming his dream. How can she avoid it without simply giving up speaking, leaving authority to men and phallocentrism?

She begins the transcribed seminar with this introduction: 'There are questions that I don't really see how I could answer. In any case "simply"' (*Ce Sexe,* p. 120). She can respond to a question, give associations, keep talking, hopefully continue to interrogate. But she 'doesn't see', has a blind spot which she exposes: her inability to give a 'simple' answer, a unified, definitive answer, the kind valorized by an ideology of well-framed representation. She is inadequate to a phallomorphic answer. The phallus is singular ('simple'), represents a unified self, as opposed to the indefinite plurality of female genitalia (clitoris, vagina, lips—how many?, cervix, breasts—Irigaray is fond of making the list, which never has quite the same elements, never is 'simply' finished).

'In other words', she continues, 'I don't know how to conduct here some *renversement* [overthrow/reversal] of the pedagogic relation in which, holding a truth about woman, a theory of woman, I could answer your questions: answer for woman in front of you.' The pedagogic relation expects her as 'authority' to have a 'truth', a 'theory' which would allow her to 'simply' answer. She would then 'answer for woman', speak for her not as her. Woman would be the subject-matter, the material of her discourse. She would trade woman, just as women have always been 'merchandise' in a commerce between men. Woman is passed from the hands of the father to the husband, from the pimp to the john, from the professor to the student who asks questions about the riddle of femininity.

There is a certain pederasty implicit in pedagogy. A greater man penetrates a lesser man with his knowledge. The *homo*sexuality means that both are measurable by the same standards, by which measure one is greater than the other. Irigaray uncovers a sublimated male homosexuality structuring all our institutions: pedagogy, marriage, commerce, even Freud's theory of so-called heterosexuality. Those structures necessarily exclude women, but are unquestioned because sublimated—raised from suspect homo*sexuality* to secure homo*logy*, to the sexually indifferent *logos*, science, logic.

But what of Irigaray's phrase: 'I don't know how to conduct here some *renversement* of the pedagogic relation'? Again she is admitting, from the position of supposed knowledge, her inadequacy—'I don't know.' That already is a reversal of the pedagogic relation. The teacher 'knows', the student does not. But what Irigaray does not know is how to reverse the relation, how to get out of the position of authority. Her lack of knowledge is specifically her inability to speak her lack of knowledge, her inability to make a non-phallic representation. Of course there is also the sense that a woman in the role of authority is already a reversal. But she cannot carry off that reversal, cannot profess about women, cannot 'simply' theorize. 'Renversement' means both 'reversal' and 'overthrow'. The pedagogic relation ought to be overthrown, but this subversion tends to be a reversal, which would bring us back to the same. If men and women, teachers and students switched places, there would still be an economy of symmetry, in which the knowledge of the one, the theory of the one, was the gauge for measuring the worth of the other, still no dialogue between two different sexes, knowledges, only a homologue with one side lacking what the other has.

'I will thus not bring definitions into a questioned discourse.' She does not know what to do to bring about an upset of the pedagogic, pederastic relation, but she can decide what not to do. She refuses definitions, definiteness which fixes plurality into unified representations. She will not bring definitions from outside into a 'questioned discourse'. The process of questioning is a specific dialectic shattering stable assumptions and producing contextual associations. To bring in ready-made definitions as answer to questions is not really to allow one's discourse or authority to be called into question. Such prepared answers are not part of a specific dialogue, but simply immutable truth that is unaffected by dialogue. That sort of relation—the mocked-up, artificial, Socratic dialogue of pedagogy with the 'answer' prior to and independent of the question and the questioning—denies any possibility of an unsettling contact with the questioner's otherness, one that might affect definition. Good pedagogic definition remains aloof from the situation, free from the desires of student and teacher, free from desire, sexually indifferent. Irigaray's uncertain, indeterminate attempt to respond to questions without giving definitive answers thus attempts really to engage the questions, to dialogue with something *hetero* (other) rather than being trapped in the *homo* (same).

Compare Irigaray's seminar to Freud's situation in the 'lecture' on femininity. First, there is the difference between lecture and seminar, the seminar supposedly implying a plurality of contribution, whereas the lecture divides into speaker presumed to have knowledge and listeners presumed to learn—to be lacking in knowledge.[5] But as Irigaray reminds us in the first footnote of *Speculum*, 'Femininity' is a fictive lecture. In the preface to the *New Introductory Lectures*, Freud writes: 'These new lectures... have never been delivered. ....If, therefore, I once more take my place in the lecture room, it is only by an artifice of the imagination; it may help me not to forget to bear the reader in mind as I enter more deeply into my subject.'

As he 'enters more deeply into his subject', in this case as he 'enters more deeply' into woman, he needs an 'artifice of the imagination', a fantasy that he is really communicating not just trapped in his own sameness. Freud fantasizes the lecture hall so as to conjure up the comforting pederastic relation as he penetrates into femininity. Whereas Irigaray will not give answers, and publishes the questions posed by others, Freud, with the exception of the Heine fragment and its hidden questions, writes from an imaginary dialogue in which otherness is simply a fantasy, an artificial projection. Such is, according to Irigaray, the so-called heterosexual encounter: man's relation is only to his imaginary other; femininity is no more encountered as otherness and difference than in Freud's audience.

Irigaray takes Freud's fictive lecture and forces it into a dialogic context. She becomes the reader, not Freud's imagined reader, but an impertinent questioner. Although Freud begins his lecture 'Ladies and Gentlemen', a few pages later (right after the Heine poem and its shift of emphasis from woman to man), he says: 'Nor will *you* have escaped worrying over this problem, because *you* are men; as for the *women among you* this will not apply, *they* are themselves this riddle' (my italics). When he explicitly addresses the audience as sexed beings, he reserves the second person pronoun for men, and refers to women with the third person pronoun. Freud talks *to* men *about* women. I have provided my own translation because Strachey's translation (*NIL*, p. 113) covers over this telling inequity in Freud's text, using the second person pronoun for both sexes. Irigaray's 'impertinence' is her assumption of the place of Freud's interlocutor, an exclusively male position. As a woman, this lecture does not speak to her, only about her. But she speaks up, responds, breaking the homosexual symmetry.

Irigaray impertinently asks a few questions, as if the student, the women, the reader were not merely a lack waiting to be filled with Freud's knowledge, but a real interlocutor, a second viewpoint. And in her questions a certain desire comes through, not a desire for a 'simple answer', but for an encounter, a hetero-sexual dialogue. Not in the customary way we think heterosexual–the dream of symmetry, two opposite sexes complementing each other. In that dream the woman/student/reader ends up functioning as mirror, giving back a coherent, framed representation to the appropriately masculine subject. There is no real sexuality of the *heteros*. 'Will there ever be any relation between the sexes?' –asks Irigaray (*Speculum*, p. 33).

Irigaray's reading of Freud seeks that 'relation between the sexes'. Her aggression is not merely some man-hating, penis-envying urge to destroy the phallocentric oppressor. She lays fiery siege to the Phallus, out of a yearning to get beyond its prohibitiveness and touch some masculine body. It is the rule of the Phallus as standard for any sexuality which denigrates women, and makes any relation between the sexes impossible, any relation between two modalities of desire, between two desires unthinkable. The rule of the Phallus is the reign of the One, of Unicity. In the 'phallic phase', according to Freud, 'only one kind of genital organ comes into account–the male'.[6] Freud, man, is arrested in the phallic phase, caught in the reign of the One, obsessively trying to tame otherness in a mirror-image of sameness.

In the transcribed seminar, Irigaray says: 'What I desire and what I am waiting for, is what men will do and say if their sexuality gets loose from the empire of phallocratism' (*Ce Sexe*, pp. 133–4). The masculine exists no more than does the feminine.

The specificity of both is suppressed by the reign of the Idea, the Phallus. Freud is not without a certain awareness of this. Something like the trace of a non-phallic masculinity can be read in a footnote that appears a few sentences after his statement about 'one kind of genital organ': 'It is remarkable, by the way, what a small degree of interest the other part of the male genitals, the little sac with its contents, arouses in the child. From all one hears in analyses one could not guess that the male genitals consist of anything more than the penis.' 'By the way', in a remark marginal to the central thrust of his argument can be found that which must be left aside by phallocentrism. Yet it is precisely because of the anatomical discrepancies in 'all one hears in analysis' that analysis can be the place where the untenable reductions that constitute the reign of the phallus are most noticeable.

The difference, of course, between the phallic suppression of masculinity and the phallic suppression of femininity is that the phallic represents (even if inaccurately) the masculine and not the feminine. By giving up their bodies, men gain power—the power to theorize, to represent themselves, to exchange women, to reproduce themselves and mark their offspring with their name. All these activities ignore bodily pleasure in pursuit of representation, reproduction, production. 'In this "phallocratic" power, man is not without loss: notably in regard to the enjoyment of his body' (*Ce Sexe*, p. 140).

Irigaray's reading of Freud's theory continually discovers an ignoring of pleasure. The theory of sexuality is a theory of the sexual function (ultimately the reproductive function) and questions of pleasure are excluded, because they have no place in an economy of production. Commenting on Freud's discussion of breast-feeding, Irigaray remarks: 'Every consideration of pleasure in nursing appears here to be excluded, unrecognized, prohibited. That, certainly, would introduce some nuances in such statements' (*Speculum*, p. 13). A consideration of pleasure would introduce a few nuances into the theory ('nuance', from *nue*, cloud). A consideration of pleasure might cloud the theory, cloud the view, reduce its ability to penetrate with clarity, to appropriate. The distinction of active and passive roles becomes more ambiguous when it is a question of pleasure. And it is the distinction active/passive which is in question in Freud's discussion of nursing.

Freud writes: 'A mother is active in every sense towards the child; the act of nursing itself may equally be described as the mother suckling the baby or as her being sucked by it' (*NIL*, p. 115). The sentence seems contradictory. If a mother is so clearly 'active in every sense', why is the only example chosen so easily interpretable as either active or passive? The difficulty is symptomatic of one of the most insistent problems for Freud—the relation of the dichotomies active/passive and masculine/feminine. According to Freud, the opposition active/passive characterizes the anal phase, whereas masculine/feminine is the logic of adult sexuality. In this discussion of the mother Freud is trying to show how improper it is to identify feminine with passive, masculine with active, since a mother is clearly feminine and clearly active. Again and again in different books and articles over a span of twenty years,[7] Freud will try to differentiate and articulate the anal dichotomy and the adult sexual opposition. Without much success.

In 'Femininity' Freud refers to the confusion of these two oppositions as 'the error of superimposition'. The footnote to the English translation indicates that such an error consists in 'mistaking two different things for a single one' (*NIL*, p. 115). Thus 'the error of superimposition' is emblematic of what Irigaray finds as the general 'error' of Freud's sexual theory—mistaking two different sexes for a single one.

In the French translation of the text,[8] 'Überdeckungsfehler' ('the error of superimposition') becomes 'l'erreur de raisonnement analogique', 'the error of analogical reasoning'. The specific superimposition in this text is both analogical and anal-logical. Anal logic organizes everything according to the opposition active/passive. The phrase 'analogical reasoning' ties the whole problematic of defining sexual difference in a non-anal logic to another persistent embarrassment. For Freud, analogy is dangerously seductive. In 1905 he writes: 'Shall we not *yield to the temptation* to construct [the formation of a joke] on the analogy of the formation of a dream?' In 1937: 'I have not been able to *resist the seduction* of an analogy'.[9] Is not the guilty compulsion to analogy symptomatic of Freud's inability to escape anal logic?

Irigaray suggests that Freud's model of sexuality has a strong anal erotic bias. The faeces become other products (a baby, a penis, a representation, a theory)[10] but the emphasis is on the product. Why else would the ambiguous nursing (describable in either active or passive terms) be so clearly an 'activity'? Indeed breast-feeding constitutes the model of the Freudian oral phase, which is defined as prior to the opposition active/passive. Freud's anal logic thus even intrudes into the very stage defined as pre-anal. In this case, the inconsistency cannot be explained as a legacy in a later stage from the earlier anal period. We are faced with the anal fixation of the theory itself.

An accusation of contradiction could be levelled at this point. Earlier in the present text Freud has been deemed 'arrested in the phallic phase'. Now he is judged 'arrested' in the anal phase. It is not a question of resolving this contradiction, of fixing the diagnosis of Freud's personal pathology. Freud himself acknowleged that the stages of development are not clearly separate and distinct. The attempt to isolate each stage could be considered an effect to reduce sexuality to only one modality at any given moment, symptomatic of the rule of the One.

The investment in unicity, in one sexuality, shows itself in Freud's description of the little girl 'in the phallic phase'. (Of course, the very assimilation of the girl into a *phallic* phase is already a sign of 'an error of superimposition', analogical reasoning.) Freud insists that, in the phallic phase, little girls only get pleasure from their clitoris and are unfamiliar with the rest of their genitalia. (Remember the phallic phase is characterized as recognizing only one kind of sexual organ.) Yet others have found girls at this stage aware of vaginal sensations, and Freud dismisses this peremptorily as well as somewhat contradictorily: 'It is true that there are a few isolated reports of early vaginal sensations as well, but it could not be easy to distinguish these from sensations in the anus or vestibulum; *in any case they cannot play a great part*. We are *entitled to keep our view* that in the phallic phase of girls the clitoris is the leading erotogenic zone' (*NIL*, p. 118, italics mine). Why 'can they not play a great part'? Because then 'we' would not be 'entitled to keep our *view*', keep our *theoria*. Entitled by what or whom? The blind spot is obvious; what must be protected is 'our view', appropriate to the masculine.

Freud insists on reducing the little girl's genitalia to her clitoris because that organ fits 'our view', is phallomorphic, can be measured by the same standard (*summetros*). 'We are now obliged to recognize that the little girl is a little man' (*NIL*, p. 118), declares Freud, making the phallocentric pederastic economy clear. The girl is assimilated to a male model, male history and, 'naturally', found lacking. The condition of that assimilation is the reduction of any possible complexity, plural sexuality, to the one, the simple, in this case to the phallomorphic clitoris.

Once reduced to phallomorphic measures, woman is defined as 'really castrated', by Freud/man. As such she is the guarantee against man's castration anxiety. She has no desires that don't complement his, so she can mirror him, provide him with a representation of himself which calms his fears and phobias about (his own potential) otherness and difference, about some 'other view' which might not support his narcissistic overinvestment in his penis. 'As for woman, *on peut se demander* [one could wonder, ask oneself] why she submits so easily. . . to the counter-phobic projects, projections, productions of man relative to his desire' (*Speculum*, p. 61).

The expression for wondering, for speculation, which Irigaray uses above, is the reflexive verb 'se demander', literally 'to ask oneself'. Most of the 'impertinent questions' in *Speculum* seem to be addressed to Freud, or men, or the reader. But this question of woman's easy submission she must ask herself. And the answer is not so obvious. A little later, she attempts to continue this line of questioning: 'And why does she lend herself to it so easily? Because she's suggestible? Hysterical? But one can catch sight of the vicious circle' (*Speculum*, p. 69). This question of the complicity, the suggestibility of the hysteric who 'finally says in analysis [what is not] foreign to what she is expected to say there' (*Speculum*, p. 64) leads us to the contemplation of another vicious circle–the (hysterical) daughter's relationship to the father (of psychoanalysis).

The daughter's desire for her father is desperate: 'the only redemption of her value as a girl would be to seduce the father, to draw from him the mark if not the admission of some interest' (*Speculum*, p. 106). If the phallus is the standard of value, then the Father, possessor of the phallus, must desire the daughter in order to give her value. But the Father is a man (a little boy in the anal, the phallic phase) and cannot afford to desire otherness, an other sex, because that opens up his castration anxiety. The father's refusal to seduce the daughter, to be seduced by her (seduction wreaking havoc with anal logic and its active/passive distribution), gains him another kind of seduction (this one more one-sided, more like violation), a veiled seduction in the form of the law. The daughter submits to the father's rule, which prohibits the father's desire, the father's penis, out of the desire to seduce the father by doing his bidding and thus pleasing him.

That is the vicious circle. The daughter desires a heterosexual encounter with the father, and is rebuffed by the rule of the homo-logical, raising the homo over the hetero, the logical over the sexual, decreeing neither the hetero nor the sexual worthy of the father. Irigaray would like really to respond to Freud, provoke him into a real dialogue. But the only way to seduce the father, to avoid scaring him away, is to please him, and to please him one must submit to his law which proscribes any sexual relation.

Patriarchal law, the law of the father, decrees that the 'product' of sexual union, the child, shall belong exclusively to the father, be marked with his name. Also that the womb which bears that child should be a passive receptacle with no claims on the product, the womb 'itself possessed as a means of (re)production' (*Speculum*, p. 16). Irigaray understands woman's exclusion from production via a reading of Marx and Engels which she brings in as a long association near the end of her reading of Freud's dream. That exclusion of the woman is inscribed in her relation to the father. Any feminist upheaval, which would change woman's definition, identity, name as well as the foundations of her economic status, must undo the vicious circle by which the desire for the father's desire (for his penis) causes her to submit to the father's law, which denies his desire/penis, but operates in its place, and according to Irigaray, even procures for him a surplus of pleasure.

The question of why woman complies must be asked. To ask that question is to ask what woman must not do anymore, what feminist strategy ought to be. Only a fool would wait for an answer, deferring the struggle against phallocentrism until a definitive explanation were found. In lieu of that 'answer', I would like slowly to trace a reading of a section of *Speculum* which concerns the father and the daughter, in this case specifically the father of psychoanalysis and his hysterics, but also the father of psychoanalytic theory and his daughter Irigaray.

Irigaray reads in Freud an account of an episode from the beginnings of psychoanalysis which '*caused [him] many distressing hours*' (Irigaray's italics): 'In the period in which the main interest was directed to discovering infantile sexual traumas, almost all my woman patients told me that they had been seduced by their father. I was driven to recognize in the end, that these reports were untrue and so came to understand that hysterical

symptoms are derived from phantasies and not from real occur-
rences' (*NIL*, p. 120; *Speculum*, p. 40). Irigaray suggests that the
reader 'imagine that x, of the masculine gender, of a ripe age,
uses the following language, how would you interpret it: "it
caused me many distressing hours", "almost all *my* woman
patients told *me* that they had been seduced by their *father*."'
Irigaray invites her reader to interpret Freud. She does not offer a
definitive reading, closing the text, making it her property, but
only notes those phrases which seem interpretable, drawing the
rebus but not giving the solution, so as to induce her reader to
play analyst.

'And let us leave the interpretation to the discretion of each
analyst, be she/he improvised for the occasion. It would even be
desirable if she/he were, otherwise he/she would risk having
already been seduced, whatever her/his sex, or her/his gender,
by the *father* of psychoanalysis' (pp. 40–1, Irigaray's italics). The
reader is considered an analyst and capable of his/her own interpretation. But Irigaray recognizes that 'the analyst' in question
may not 'really' be a psychoanalyst, but rather be the recipient of
a sort of battlefield promotion, prepared only by the experience
of reading Freud with Irigaray. *Speculum* becomes a 'training
analysis', the reading of it preparing the reader to make her/his
own interpretations. And the analyst trained by *Speculum* is
likely to be a better analyst of Freud than a proper psychoanalyst,
for any analyst—male or female, masculine or feminine, *Irigaray
herself*—is likely to have been seduced by Freud, seduced by his
theory.

There is a contrast here between two different kinds of analyst. The one privileged by Irigaray is an amateur, a 'wild
analyst',[11] not 'entitled' to analyze, but simply a reader, who can
catch symptoms and make her/his own interpretations. The
other sort of analyst is a professional, which is to say has invest-
ments in analysis as an identity and an economically productive
system, and a transference onto Freud, that is, a belief in Freud's
knowledge. The analyst is likely to 'see' according to Freud's
theory, having been seduced into sharing 'our view', giving a
predictable 'Freudian' interpretation, one that always hears according to the same standards, returning every text to pre-existent
Freudian models, 'bringing definitions into a discourse from
outside'. Irigaray as an analyst is perhaps not as likely to give an
attentive, specific interpretation as is her reader. So that, once

again, as in the *Ce Sexe* seminar, she proceeds to some sort of overthrow of a certain hierarchy between theoretical writer as distributor of knowledge and reader as passive, lacking consumer.

But certain questions pose themselves to this reader at this point. Can Irigaray really overthrow the pedagogic relation, or is this merely a ruse to flatter the reader into less resistance, a ploy to seduce her reader? For she *does* go on to interpret, simply having deferred it for a few sentences. As in an artificial, Socratic (pederastic) dialogue, if she asks the reader to think for him/her self, that reader will produce an answer which the teacher expected all along, the right answer. Like Freud in the *New Introductory Lectures*, Irigaray is fantasizing a reader, one who would make the same associations as she does, one created in her own image.

It is thus interesting that at this point Irigaray is reasoning by analogy—Freud: hysteric :: father : daughter :: Freud : any other psychoanalyst. Analogy, as Irigaray has said, is one of the 'eternal operations which support the defining of difference in function of the a priori of the same' (*Speculum*, p. 28). The analogy of analyst to father is the analytic analogy *par excellence*, the fact of transference. Transference is the repetition of infantile prototype relations, of unconscious desires in the analytic relation. Without transference, psychoanalysis is simply literary criticism, by an unimplicated, discriminating reader, lacking either affect or effect.

The example of *the* analytic analogy suggests a way of overturning the phallocentric effects of analogy. Analogy cannot simply be avoided, it is radically tempting. Transference occurs everywhere, not just in psychoanalysis but in any relation where the other is 'presumed to know', relations to teachers, loved ones, doctors. But psychoanalysis provides the opportunity to analyze the transference, take cognizance of it as such and work it through. Likewise Irigaray's use of analogy in a context where analogy has been analyzed provides a way of making the economic function of analogy evident. The phallocentric effect of analogy would be explicit, and thus less powerful.

Her use of analogy as well as her projection of a reader in her own image, a narcissistic mirror, means she has acceded to a certain economy of the homo...and the auto..., the economy which men have and women are excluded from. Of course, the 'answer' is not to set up another homosexual economy, but that may be necessary as one step to some hetero-sexuality. 'Of course, it is not a question, in the final analysis, of demanding the *same* attributions. Still it is necessary that women arrive at the same so that consideration be made, be imposed of the differences that they would elicit there' (*Speculum*, pp. 148–9). Women need to reach 'the same': that is, be 'like men', able to represent themselves. But they also need to reach 'the same', 'the homo': their own homosexual economy, a female homosexuality that ratifies and glorifies female standards. The two 'sames' are inextricably linked. Female homosexuality, when raised to an ideology, tends to be either masculine (women that are 'like men') or essentialistic (based on some ascertainable female identity). The latter is as phallic as the former for it reduces heterogeneity to a unified, rigid representation. But without a female homosexual economy, a female narcissistic ego, a way to represent herself, a woman in a heterosexual encounter will always be engulfed by the male homosexual economy, will not be able to represent her difference. Woman must demand 'the same', 'the homo' and then not settle for it, not fall into the trap of thinking a female 'homo' is necessarily any closer to a representation of otherness, an opening for the other.

Yet having posed these questions of Irigaray's own imaginary economy, I might also say she was right about her reader. Her fantasized reader would be the impertinent questioner she is. I am asking Irigaray Irigarayan questions, reopening the interrogation when Luce becomes too tight, when she seems to settle on an answer. I have been seduced into a transference onto her, into following her suggestion, into saying 'what is not foreign to what I am expected to say', into playing 'wild analysis'.

'This seduction', she continues, 'is covered of course, in practice or theory, by a normative statement, by a *law*, which denies it.' A new element is introduced by Irigaray and emphasized: the law. This term, foreign to the Freud passage she is reading, not suggested by him, is Irigaray's own association, her remaining in excess of the Freudian seduction. 'Law' is a political term, refers to patriarchy, the law of the father, and here will refer to Freud's legislative control of his theory, his normative prescriptions.

Her text continues with another sentence from Freud: 'It was only later that I was able to recognize in the phantasy of being seduced by the father *the expression of the typical Oedipus complex* in women' (*NIL*, p. 120; *Speculum*, p. 41, Irigaray's italics). The seduction by the father is not only a mere fantasy, but is the manifestation of a typical complex, one that is supposed to be universal, and therefore a law of Freudian theory. Given Irigaray's introduction to this passage, we read that the Oedipus complex, the incest taboo, the law forbidding intercourse between father and daughter, covers over a seduction, masks it so it goes unrecognized. Also covered over is a seduction in the theory, whereby psychoanalysts through their transference onto Freud (their unfulfillable desire for his love and approval) accept his immutable theoretical laws.

'It would be too risky, it seems, to admit that the father could be a seducer, and even eventually that he desires to have a daughter *in order to* seduce her. That he wishes to become an analyst in order to exercise by hypnosis, suggestion, transference, interpretation bearing on the sexual economy, on the proscribed, prohibited sexual representations, a *lasting seduction upon the hysteric*' (Irigaray's italics) (p. 41). Freud as a father must deny the possibility of being seductive. Patriarchy is grounded in the uprightness of the father. If he were devious and unreliable, he could not have the power to legislate. The law is supposed to be just—that is, impartial, indifferent, free from desire.

'It is necessary to endure the law which exculpates the operation. But, of course, if under cover of the law the seduction can now be practised at leisure, it appears just as urgent to interrogate *the seductive function of the law itself*' (Irigaray's italics) (p. 41). For example, the law which prohibits sexual intercourse between analyst and patient actually makes the seduction last forever. The sexually actualized seduction would be complicitous, nuanced, impossible to delineate into active and passive roles, into the anal logic so necessary for a traditional distribution of wealth and power. But the 'lasting seduction' of the law is never consummated and as such maintains the power of the prohibited analyst. The seduction which the daughter desires would give her contact with the father as masculine sexed body. The seduction which the father of psychoanalysis exercises refuses her his body, his penis, and asks her to embrace his law, his indifference, his phallic uprightness.

Psychoanalysis works because of the transference, which is to say because the hysteric transfers her desire to seduce her father, to be seduced by him, onto her analyst. But since the fantasy of seducing the father is produced in analysis, it is produced for the

analyst. In order to please him, in order to seduce him, in order
to give him what he wants. The installation of the law in psychoanalysis, the prohibition of the analyst's penis by the Doctor in a
position to validate the hysteric, to announce her as healthy, sets
up the desperate situation outlined by Irigaray: 'the only
redemption of her value as a girl would be to seduce the father'
(*Speculum*, p. 106).

'Thus is it not simply true, nor on the other hand completely
false, to claim that the little girl fantasizes being seduced by her
father, because it is just as pertinent to admit that *the father
seduces his daughter* but that, refusing to recognize and realize
his desire—not always it is true—, *he legislates to defend himself
from it*' (*Speculum*, p. 41, Irigaray's italics). The father's law is a
counterphobic mechanism. He must protect himself from his
desire for the daughter. His desire for the feminine threatens his
narcissistic overvaluation of his penis. It is so necessary to deny his
attraction for the little girl that Freud denies her existence: 'We
must admit that the little girl is a little man.' If the father were to
desire his daughter he could no longer exchange her, no longer
possess her in the economy by which true, masterful possession is
the right to exchange. If you cannot give something up for something of like value, if you consider it nonsubstitutable, then you
do not possess it any more than it possesses you. So the father
must not desire the daughter for that threatens to remove him
from the homosexual commerce in which women are exchanged
between men, in the service of power relations and community
for the men.

Also: if the father desires his daughter as daughter he will be
outside his Oedipal desire for his mother, which is to say also
beyond 'the phallic phase'. So the law of the father protects him
and patriarchy from the potential havoc of the daughter's desirability. Were she recognized as desirable in her specificity as
daughter, not as son ('little man') nor as mother, there would be a
second sexual economy besides the one between 'phallic little boy'
and 'phallic mother'. An economy in which the stake might not
be a reflection of the phallus, the phallus's desire for itself.

'In place of the desire for the sexed body of the father there
thus comes *to be proposed, to be imposed, his law*, that is to say
an institutionalizing and institutionalized discourse. In part,
defensive (Think of those "distressing hours"...)' (pp. 41–2,
Irigaray's italics). The father gives his daughter his law and pro-

tects himself from her desire for his body, protects himself from his body. For it is only the law–and not the body–which constitutes him as patriarch. Paternity is corporeally uncertain, without evidence. But patriarchy compensates for that with the law which marks each child with the father's name as his exclusive property.

'That is not to say that the father *should* make love with his daughter–from time to time it is better to state things precisely– but that it would be good to call into question this mantle of the law with which he drapes his desire, and his sex (organ)' (p. 42, Irigaray's italics). The strategic difference between a prescriptive 'should' and a suggestive 'it would be good' is emphasized by this sentence. But suggestion may have always been a more devious, more powerful mode of prescription.

'It would be good' to question the law's appearance of indifference, as Irigaray questions it, and find the phallic stake behind it. 'It would be good' to lift 'the mantle of the law' so that the father's desire and his penis are exposed. But that does not mean the 'answer' is for the father to make love to his daughter. Irigaray, above all, avoids giving an answer, a prescription such as 'the father *should* make love with his daughter'. Not that he might not, not that it might not be a way to lift the law and expose the sexed body. The 'should' is underlined, because that is what Irigaray will not say. She will not lay down a law about how to lift the law.

If she did lay down such a law–'the father should make love with his daughter'–it would, like all laws, mask and support a desire. The negated appearance of this law suggests the mechanism Freud called *Verneinung*–'Procedure whereby the subject, while formulating one of his wishes, thoughts or feelings which has been repressed hitherto, contrives, by disowning it, to continue to defend himself against it.'[12] What surfaces that Irigaray needs to disown is her desire to impose the law upon the father, her desire for a simple reversal rather than an overthrow of patriarchy.

This sentence is marked as symptomatic, asking for analysis, by the parenthetical remark, 'from time to time it is better to state things precisely'. 'From time to time' pretends this is a random moment; it just happens to fall at this moment that she will be precise. But this is the only such remark in all of her reading of Freud; this is the point where she is most afraid of a misunderstanding. Her desire to be precise is in direct contradiction to something she says later in *Speculum* about feminist strategies of language: 'No clear nor univocal statement can, in fact, dissolve this mortgage, this obstacle, all of them being caught, trapped, in the same reign of credit. It is as yet better to speak only through equivocations, allusions, innuendos, parables... Even if you are asked for some *précisions* [precise details]' (*Speculum*, p. 178). All clear statements are trapped in the same economy of values, in which clarity (oculocentrism) and univocity (the One) reign. Precision must be avoided, if the economy of the One is to be unsettled. Equivocations, allusions, etc. are all flirtatious; they induce the interlocutor to listen, to encounter, to interpret, but defer the moment of assimilation back into a familiar model. Even if someone asks for *précisions*, even if that someone is oneself, it is better for women to avoid stating things precisely.

Yet on one point Luce Irigaray tightens up, prefers to be precise, to return to an economy of clarity and univocity. The locus of her conservatism, her caution, her need to defend herself, is the question of making love with the father. It is terrifying to lift the mantle of the law and encounter the father's desire. What if in making love the father still remained the law, and the daughter were just passive, denied? The father's law has so restructured the daughter and her desires that it is hard, well nigh impossible, to differentiate the Father (that is to say, the Law) from the male sexed body. What if making love with the father were merely a ruse to get the impertinent daughter to give up her resistance to the law?

Irigaray clutches for something stable, something precise, because she too is a 'subject', with a stake in identity. And the law of the father gives her an identity, even if it is not her own, even if it blots out her feminine specificity. To give it up is not a 'simple' matter. It must be done over and over.

Later she will say of her method in *Speculum*, 'what was left for me to do was to *have an orgy with the philosophers*' (*Ce Sexe*, p. 147, Irigaray's italics). Intercourse with the philosophers, the father of psychoanalysis included, is her method of insinuation into their system, of inducing them to reveal the phallocentrism, the desire cloaked in their sexual indifference. Perhaps these are merely two different moments in her inconsistency: a brave, new, loose moment—'have an orgy with the philosophers'—and a defensive, cautious moment—refusal to make love with the father.

But perhaps these are not merely two moments. The two situations are *analogous, but not the same*. Some terms may be more frightening, more sensitive than others. 'Father' may be more threatening than 'philosophers'. She writes in *Ce Sexe*: 'As far as the family is concerned, *my answer will be simple* and clear: the family has always been the privileged locus of the exploitation of women. Thus, as far as familialism is concerned, there is no ambiguity!' (pp. 139–40, my italics). Yet earlier in the same text she says she cannot give a 'simple answer'. Also: 'faire l'amour' (make love) may be more threatening than 'faire la noce' (have an orgy). Maybe what frightens her is not seduction of the father or by the father but 'making love'. 'Love' has always been sublimated, idealized desire, away from the bodily specificity and towards dreams of complementarity, and the union of opposites, difference resolved into the One. 'Love' is entangled with the question of woman's complicity; it may be the bribe which has persuaded her to agree to her own exclusion. It may be historically necessary to be momentarily blind to father-love; it may be politically effective to defend–tightly, unlucidly–against its inducements, in order for a 'relation between the sexes', in order to rediscover some feminine desire, some desire for a masculine body that does not re-spect the Father's law.

6 Impertinent Questions

The Freud Irigaray both uses and questions is based on Jacques Lacan's reading of Freud. After *Speculum* and her encounter with Freud, she mounts a campaign or two against Lacan–'Cosi fan tutti' and 'La "Mécanique" des fluides' (both found in *Ce Sexe qui n'en est pas un*). Irigaray wants to interrogate ghosts: specifically, to question the 'phantoms' whose reflections cannot be seen in Lacan's famous mirror. In one of the earliest of his writings ('Le Stade du miroir' in *Écrits*), Lacan explains the mirror-stage as the moment when the infant proleptically takes on a totalizing/totalized shape–a cohesive identity–through the mediation of a mirror and, more importantly, the Other (embodied, for example, by the mother). This alienation in the constitution of a self, Lacan and Irigaray agree, will later serve as the basis for the alienation of the specular self in the social self. Irigaray, however, considers that 'it is appropriate to question oneself about the status of the "exteriority" of this constituting shape... and about the phantoms [the shape] leaves behind' ('Mecanique', pp. 114–15). She is interested in questioning what is left out, not properly buried and contained, by the necessity of constituting a well-composed, presentable self. And at the very moment she is wondering about such ghosts, a phantom appears–one that has been excluded from Irigaray's own well-articulated polemic position. In the paragraph preceding the above quotation, she has written: 'A substantial homage is owed here for this recognition by a master of specular profit and "alienation." But too flat an ad-miration risks suspending the efficacy of this step beyond.' 'Too flat an ad-miration' might undermine Irigaray's own 'step beyond' Lacan.

Hommage: 'the act by which the vassal declares himself the *man* of his lord', from *homme*: 'an individual considered as dependent upon another, under his authority' (*Le Petit Robert* dictionary). The risk in this homage is that she will become Lacan's man. That would be 'too flat an ad-miration', too flat a mirroring, the Man's mirror v. Irigaray's speculum. Her curving of the mirror is a small but efficient step beyond. For fear that subtle step be reappropriated by the lord and master, she refuses to honour her debt, refuses to honour his name.

The entire collection of essays, *Ce Sexe qui n'en est pas un*, continually works to dig out of debt, out of the property/debt/ gift system, the circuit of exchange which includes Lévi-Strauss's exchange of women (see 'Le Marché des femmes' in *Ce Sexe*). Any gift or debt alienates the individual into the circuit of exchanges, compromises one's integrity and autonomy. But assertion of one's uncontaminated selfhood is no practical way out of the circuit.

Alienation is the necessary obverse of the self's integrity. Violation would lose its meaning and its attraction were the body no longer represented as 'virginal-solid-closed, to be opened with violence' (*Ce Sexe*, p. 199). The economy of phallic desire is subtended by a notion of woman as property belonging to the man whose name she bears, and the penetration of her? his? body is an act of breaking and entering. Even if a woman's body were her own, the problem/attraction of rape would not disappear. The social self (self tainted by the world) is grounded in the specular self (assumption of the fictionally solid, cohesive body— total shape, well-defined and firm). Alienation/violation cannot be avoided without calling into question the specular self, the fictional unity of the body. The answer to woman as property is *not* the restoration to woman of her body, her self.

Irigaray characterizes the economy founded upon a self un-compromised by any exchange with the economic term 'autarky' (*Ce Sexe*, p. 206). 'Autarky' is 'a policy of self-sufficiency and non-reliance on imports or economic aid'. Irigaray does not want to exclude exchange, rather she dreams of 'exchanges without commerce' (p. 213). That phrase appears in a lyrical essay in *Ce Sexe*, entitled 'Quand nos lèvres se parlent' (When our lips speak to each other), an exhilarating text lacking the polemic defen-siveness of the pieces on Lacan. 'When our lips speak to each other': whose lips (plural even in one body), not to mention which lips, speak to whose (which)? The dialogue is already four or eight or twelve; and the tight reciprocity of the verb 'se parler' is opened up to some pretty juicy exchanges.

Of course the phallic economy never has actually worked neatly and efficiently. Phantoms always lurk, messing up (phantoms of violence can be bloody) 'the fantasy of virginal-solid-closed body'.

Sexual commerce is obstructed and difficult. But, Irigaray finds, someone is profiteering from this general economic failure.

Irigaray calls one of her articles on Lacan 'Cosi fan tutti', thus recalling Mozart's opera, in which Don Alfonso, the cynical old philosopher, knows all about women. He tells two naive young men that they should not trust women, that communication between the sexes is unreliable. They do not believe him; so he sets up a wager to prove his point. The young men trick their women into proving unfaithful, and because of the trick the two couples end up happily together in misunderstanding. But the real winner is the old man who profits–wins a bet of 100 sovereigns–and is proven wise from the failure of trustworthy exchange between the sexes.[1] The sarcastic old analyst, like the cynical old philosopher, supports the intolerable sexual economy (which he lucidly/ludicly recognizes as intolerable), because he capitalizes on this failing commerce, garnering knowledge as surplus value. He's the one who knows, who knows it does not work. 'Cosi fan tutti' begins with the following quotation from Lacan: 'He whom I presume to have knowledge, he's the one I love.'

Lacan is not the only character in *Ce Sexe* whose speculations on sexual commerce gain him a 'premium of pleasure in knowledge' ('Cosi', p. 91). In the article, '"Françaises", ne faites plus un effort...'–an article on pornographic scenes in which the young girl is initiated into sexual practice–Irigaray writes: 'And that women remain *mute* and *always and still ignorant* about [their] *jouissance* [enjoyment, orgasm], who will be surprised?... That the libertine, thanks to their *jouissance*, knows a little more [about "nature"], such is *his* premium of pleasure' (p. 198, Irigaray's italics). Two quotations from Lacan begin 'Cosi fan tutti': 'He whom I presume to have knowledge, he's the one I love' and 'Women don't know what they're saying, that's all the difference between them and me.'

The libertine and the analyst gain knowledge (love, pleasure, power) while women are ignorant about themselves. However, just as 'the analyst' is not just any psychoanalyst, '"Françaises", ne faites plus un effort...'is not about just any non-specific pornographic initiation. The title, '"Frenchwomen", don't make another effort...'is a response to the pamphlet–'Frenchmen, one more effort if you wish to be republicans'–which is inserted into Sade's *Philosophy in the Bedroom*. The pornographic scene Irigaray discusses is Sade's scene, although neither author nor title are ever mentioned. And this pamphlet in *Philosophy in the Bedroom* is also the subject of one of Lacan's *Écrits*: 'Kant avec Sade'.[2] So once more, in this essay on pornography, Irigaray is very much writing with the ghostly accompaniment of Lacan.

Rather than remain mute and ignorant, thus adding to the master's premium of pleasure, Irigaray asks both Lacan and Dolmancé (the libertine instructor in Sade's *Philosophy*) several 'impertinent questions': questions that disrupt their mastery, their science. 'It is necessary to return to "science" to ask it a few questions'–so begins 'La "Mécanique" des fluides'. In a similar fashion, '"Françaises"...'opens: 'if it happened that...I resisted or survived the ascendancy of this sovereign authority, I would risk asking the libertine master a few questions'. Refusing to be overwhelmed by male expertise and technique (Lacan's discourse, Dolmancé's scientific tongue), Irigaray observes that the phallic conception of nature excludes 'certain properties of real fluids' ('Mécanique', p. 107). The logical theory of nature has been erected on solid, dry ground. Irigaray breaks up that solidity ('the long-standing solidarity of rationality and an exclusive mechanics of solids'–ibid.) and irrigates the dry field of both libertine and psychoanalytic science.

Fluidity has its own properties. It is not an inadequacy in relation to solidity. In phallic fantasy, the solid-closed-virginal body is opened with violence; and blood flows. The fluid here signifies defloration, wound as proof of penetration, breaking and entering, property damage. 'The libertine loves blood. At least that which flows according to *his* techniques. For, whatever his libertinage, his transgression of all (?) prohibitions, *menstrual blood remains generally taboo for him*' ('Françaises', p. 199, Irigaray's italics). Menstrual blood is not a wound in the closure of the body; the menstrual flow ignores the distinction virgin/ deflowered. 'To be a virgin comes down to not yet being marked by and for them. Not yet woman by and for them' (*Ce Sexe*, p. 211). The white virgin is necessarily sullied from without. In sadistic science there is no place for menstrual blood, for the latter marks woman as woman (virgin or not) with no need of man's tools.

In *Philosophy in the Bedroom*, Mme de Saint-Ange announces that in her twelve years of marriage her husband has asked for the same thing every day: that she suck his cock while shitting in his mouth. The only exception is when she has her period, then she is replaced by 'a very pretty girl'.[3] Periods are banished from this neat closed circuit of exchange. The replacement is 'very pretty', that is, well-composed and socially presentable. And this is hardly a prissy man, fussy and fearful of the flesh. Dolmancé assures us that Saint-Ange's husband is 'one of the biggest libertines of his era' (ibid.). As Irigaray says: 'Excrement, certainly, but blood from a period, no' ('Françaises', p. 199).

In 'Mécanique', Irigaray remarks on the same exclusion in psychoanalytic theory. The list of objects of desire in Lacanian theory does not include bodily fluids. The paradigm of the Lacanian object of desire is the turd, solid and countable as money. Lacan and the Sadian libertine, like Freud, are trapped in an anal–phallic phase; their infantile science sees the aim of phallic desire according to the anal model.

Irigaray has discovered that phallic sexual theory, male sexual science, is homosexual, a sexuality of sames, of identities, excluding otherness. Heterosexuality, once it is exposed as an exchange of women between men, reveals itself as a mediated form of homosexuality. All penetration, considered to be sadistic penetration of the body's defensive envelope, is thought according to the model of anal penetration. The dry anus suffers pain; the penetrated is a humiliated man. But the vagina (unknown in the phallic phase, says Freud) has a juicy receptivity which makes penetration not painful, but a free-flowing exchange, leaving no solid borders to be violated. The vagina flows before penetration. It does not wait for man to break its seal, but hospitably prepares a welcome for his entry.

The Sadian scene makes the dry/anal/homosexual ground of sexuality painfully obvious. Although directing the defloration of a girl, the master libertine is an avowed homosexual who refuses, on principle, to allow his precious penis any commerce with the fluid vagina. The solidity of his virile organ cannot risk contamination with anything so alien to it, so other that its otherness is not a specular opposite, a complement reducible to the economy of the same, but a radical other with its own properties, its own 'mechanics'.

And in its very explicitness ('excrement, certainly, but the blood of a period, no') the Sadian scene, for Irigaray, has a certain redeeming value. 'After all, it is better that the sexuality that subtends our social order be exercised overtly, than that it make its prescriptions from the place of its repressions. Maybe, by

dint of exhibiting, without shame, the phallocracy reigning everywhere, another sexual economy will become possible?' ('Françaises', p. 201). Psychoanalysis (Lacan) likewise discloses the
phallocratic truth: 'That there is no sexual relation *as such*, that
it *cannot be asserted*. One cannot but subscribe to such affirma-
tions' ('Cosi', p. 97, Irigaray's italics). But whereas she admits that
libertine science might be an improvement over the covert phallocracy of proper science/philosophy/logic, she will not make the
same concession to (Lacanian) psychoanalysis: 'Now, this discourse, like all the others, more than all the others?... perpetu-
ates the subjection of woman' (ibid., p. 101). The question–'more
than all the others?'–marks Irigaray's inquisition. Psychoanalysis
is guilty, guiltier (than Sade), guiltiest, because of its knowledge.
Because it should know better.

(Is Daddy subject to more rigorous criteria than other men?
Because the little girl once believed in him? He deceived her by
not loving her as much as she was led to expect. All men might be
horrible, but is he not the worst?)

Like Lacan, the knowledgeable libertine profits from phallocracy, in such an unabashed manner as to reveal the homosexual
closed circuit which underlies our supposed heterosexual culture.
Besides Dolmancé the other non-servant male in the story is
known simply as *Le Chevalier* (the Knight). He mouths various
humanist moral commonplaces such as sex is all right if no one is
hurt. Yet this *chivalrous* man does everything Dolmancé does,
simply giving lip service to humanism. At least Dolmancé is overt
in his anal-sadistic phallism.

Lacan too lauds the progress Sade makes by 'bringing to light
the "anal-sadistic" which clouded the subject [of the education of
young girls]' ('Kant avec Sade', p. 787). Lacan's recognition of the
value of such an exposure none the less, like Irigaray's, coexists
with disapproval for Dolmancé's attitude, a distaste for the libertine's hard-on mastery. 'There's too much preaching in it....
Despite its advantage of bringing to light the "anal-sadistic"
which clouded this subject... it remains a treatise on education.
The sermon is a deadly bore for the victim, and fatuous on the
part of the teacher' (ibid.).

Lacan rejects identification with Dolmancé because the latter
is a pious bore. Whereas Irigaray rejects Sadian pornography as
an appropriation of woman's 'nature' by phallocentrism, she does
momentarily allow that it might, after all, be an ally. Lacan who

has supposedly written this article as a preface to Sade, who wants Sade as accomplice against the fatuous and unlucid Kant, ultimately turns on Sade, lumping him with Kant, that other pious preacher. 'Already Kant, for the least little thing, could make us lose our seriousness, for lack of the slightest sense of the comic. But the one who lacks it absolutely, completely, *it has been remarked*, is Sade. This approach might be fatal to him and a preface *has not been made* to do a disservice' (ibid., p. 783), italics mine). If the strained passive construction is not a sufficient clue that this is an ironic attack on Sade, one need only turn a few pages to see that Lacan's delicate avoidance of insulting Sade is mere pretence. He goes ahead and makes the 'fatal approach' directly.

In response to Pierre Klossowski's uncovering a covert Christianity in Sade,[4] Lacan declares that it is important to remember that Sade none the less explicitly refuses Christianity (ibid., p. 789). What then must be the imagined insult when Lacan says that the problem with Sade is that he lacks the delicious and biting irony of Jesus (p. 788–Lacan cites Renan's *Life of Jesus* at length for proof).

According to Lacan, 'Sade is not close enough to his own evil to meet his fellow man there. A trait that he shares with many and notably with Freud' (p. 789). Sade is incapable of Christian charity. This statement of Sade's inadequacy is even more striking through its marriage to one of the only examples in print of Lacan directly criticizing Freud. Let us turn the tables and paraphrase: 'Lacan is not close enough to his own piousness to meet Sade there.'

(Irigaray can see Sade but not Lacan as an ally, although she classes Sade and Lacan as phallocratic colleagues. Lacan finally breaks his alliance with Sade, nearly dumping Freud in the frantic attempt to assert difference.)

Lacan bases his difference from Sade upon the famous Lacanian wit. The psychoanalyst does have one of the sharpest and nastiest senses of humour in a non-comic endeavour. But we must ask if there really is no irony, no wit in Sade's writing. We must ask if it is merely a coincidence that when Mme de Saint-Ange reveals her husband's avoidance of menstrual blood, Irigaray's sarcastic questioning–'transgression of all (?) prohibitions'–is prompted by Dolmancé's straight line: 'Madame's husband is one of the greatest libertines of his era.'

Ironically, in the very essay in which he accuses Sade of preaching, Lacan is discussing Sade's pamphlet which is itself a diatribe against religion. 'Frenchmen another effort' means that having overthrown the monarchy (*Philosophy* was written in 1796), France will still not be free unless it ousts the Church. Mere minutes before Dolmancé pulls that antireligious pamphlet out of his pocket, irritated at a young man's decidedly heterosexual preferences, the libertine master waxes philosophical in the following terms: 'That's nature: everyone preaches for his own saint' (p. 185).

Augustin worships the cunt; Dolmancé preaches for the ass. Religious terminology for sexual persuasions is rampant throughout the *Philosophy*. But the irony cuts both ways, not only debasing religion, but deriding stubborn sexual prejudice by placing it in proximity to arguments against religion and its oppressive prejudice. While the ingénue is sucking off Dolmancé, the high priest of the ass proclaims: 'Oh! delicious mouth! What warmth! . . . To me it's worth as much as the prettiest of asses! . . . Oh! Holy God! . . . Holy Fuck!' (p. 103). To which Saint-Ange calmly replies: 'how you do blaspheme, my friend.' Of course he is blaspheming in the traditional sense, but for this man to swear that a mouth rivals the ass is to take the name of his 'saint' in vain.

Perhaps Sade's text did not need to await Irigaray's embarrassing questions, impertinently exposing the phallic religion masked as libertinism. She may already be there in the character of Mme de Saint-Ange.[5] Irigaray dismisses Saint-Ange as a phallocrat, a woman who 'seduces, screws, ejaculates, strikes, even kills those weaker than she, like the strong man she is' ('Françaises', p. 198). True enough. Saint-Ange pays homage to the master, becomes his *man*. Her sexuality is male, that is quantitative. In 'Cosi fan tutti', Irigaray points out that in order to master the radical alterity of woman, men resort to the enumeration of women. The incompletion of the specular image of woman is displaced onto the need for always one more. When Saint-Ange, the phallocratic woman, is asked what is the 'most extraordinary thing she has ever done', she replies that she took on fifteen men: 'I was fucked 90 times in 24 hours, as much in front as behind' (p. 90).

Irigaray does not mention that in this education of Eugénie the ingénue, although Dolmancé might be the schoolmaster, he is commissioned by Saint-Ange. Might not Saint-Agne's goal be a tongue-in-cheek exposure of male prejudice at its most extreme?

For example, before the master arrives she confides to the *Cheva-lier*, 'I want to be the victim of his errors' (p. 12). Does she recog-nize his science as erroneous? Is she playing along for her plea-sure? Of course the signals of such ironic distance on Saint-Ange's part are few. But that may be because her resistance is not sharp irony, phallic and penetrating, not the incisive questions Irigaray would ask, but a more general irrigation, breaking up the solid ground.

(Irigaray was earlier the irrigator, now it is Saint-Ange. Am I charitable to phallocratic Saint-Ange, but expecting more from Irigaray? My 'step beyond' like any is phallic one-upmanship, re-fusing homage, refusing loyalty. Irigaray is not just my sister–rival; she is my Daddy, my Mummy. And when she is at her best, as angelic as Saint-Ange at *her* best, I love her and I get scared not knowing where the boundary lies between her and me.)

At one point, Dolmancé shows concern at Saint-Ange's ap-parent disregard for the sacredness of the anal cult–a disregard so thorough there is no need for sacrilege: 'When once one has tasted the pleasures of the ass, as you have madame, I cannot conceive [*sic*] how one can go back to other pleasures.' Saint-Ange willingly agrees, but her reply is lacking in tight, anal logic. Rather it opens up a bodily plurality that co-opts and derides Dolmancé's dogmatic monotheism. Saint-Ange: 'When you think as I do, you want to be fucked everywhere and, whatever part a tool perforates, you are happy when you feel it there. Nonetheless I am certainly of your opinion, and I will here testify to all sensu-ous women that the pleasure they experience in ass-fucking will always greatly surpass what they feel in doing it in the cunt' (pp. 141–2).

Saint-Ange is not the resistant, impertinent questioner Irigaray would be. She subtly teases Dolmancé's beliefs without his ever being alerted enough to make him hide those beliefs, which can thus be exposed in all their blind arrestment in the phallic phase. Saint-Ange's extreme light-heartedness may frighten Irigaray. The latter's refusal of Saint-Ange ('she's a phallocrat') parallels Lacan's rejection of Dolmancé ('he's fatuous'), as if both needed to assert their difference from the character they most resemble.

Having stated in 'Quand nos lèvres se parlent' that men consider women indifferent receptacles, sexual blank pages that merely bear the imprint of men, Irigaray asks, 'Doesn't that make you laugh?...Us? Indifferent?' (p. 207). Yet she adds in a nervous parenthesis (what is more nervous than a parenthetical remark, a patch-job defence?): '(If you always, and everywhere, burst into laughter, we will never be able to talk to each other. And we will still be (d)raped in their words. So let's take back a bit of our mouth to try to speak.)' If one is not phallicly militant, if one laughs at identity, how can one be certain not to be co-opted?

The following statement of tactics for revolution is found in the pamphlet 'Frenchmen another effort...': 'No, do not assassinate, do not exile: these atrocities are for kings; it is not by acting like them that you will force those who use such methods to detest them. Use force only for idols; ridicule is sufficient for those who serve them. Julien's sarcasms did more damage than all Nero's tortures' (p. 212).

Sarcasm, rather than torture: on those grounds, Lacan can declare himself more sadistic than Sade. But we also have here a revolutionary practice more effective than violence, because violence against tyrants makes us tyrants. What then is feminism to do, if not to confront and combat phallism, if not to take a position and stand solidly there? 'Quand nos lèvres se parlent' hints at another strategy: 'We are so subtle that no obstacle will resist...we pass through everything imperceptible, without ruining anything, to get together again. No one will see anything. Our force is our feeble resistance' (p. 214). Is this not Saint-Ange's strategy? And why doesn't Irigaray use it against Lacan, rather than stubbornly, defensively refusing him homage? Is it because one should 'use force for idols' although 'ridicule is sufficient for those who serve them'?

Instead of the rigid resistance of the militant virgin, Saint-Ange/Irigaray points to the disruptiveness of pliancy, prostitution of the self. The whore gives man all he wants without ever being broken, tamed, possessed; the vagina welcomes entry, expands for reception, yet regains its shape. From Saint-Ange's mouth comes this praise of floozies: 'Here are the truly loveable women, the only truly philosophical women! As for me, my dear, who for twelve years have worked to deserve [the name whore], I assure you that far from taking offence [*loin de m'en formaliser*], I enjoy it' (p. 45). The prostitute as subversive force is not she who does it for money, but the woman who, like Saint-Ange, does it for pleasure. 'Everything is exchanged, but without commerce. Between us, neither proprietors nor acquirers, no determinable objects, no prices' (*Ce Sexe*, p. 213). Saint-Ange does not *se formaliser*: that is (idiomatically), she does not take offence at the epithet whore; but also (literally), she *does not formalize herself*. By class a noble lady, she does not take on the identity prostitute; she prostitutes her identity.

Prostitution for money has a place in the phallocentric sexual economy; but the Sadian whore points to a different economy. Irigaray does wonder if perhaps Sade's exposure of 'the phallocracy reigning everywhere will make another sexual economy possible' ('Françaises', p. 201). However, she refuses Sade in the very title of her essay which warns women not to make that 'one more effort' Sade asks of them. According to Sade's pamphlet, 'it is as unjust to possess a woman exclusively as it is to possess slaves. . .no man can be excluded from the possession of a woman, as soon as it shall be seen that women belong decidedly to all men' (*Philosophy*, pp. 235–6). Irigaray rejects this sexual communism because, according to her, private property or public, woman is still property. Irigaray does not recognize here 'another sexual economy'. But Sade specifies in a footnote to the pamphlet that 'here it is only a question of enjoyment [*jouissance*] and not of property' (p. 236). The word possession is used in the sexual sense. The efficacy of Sade's formulation depends on a distinction between a theatrical, fantasmatic possession and an enduring, legal possession. Yet since the former's appeal is that it appears momentarily to be the latter, the same word must be used. An awkward footnote appended to a later statement by Dolmancé tries to make clear a similar distinction in the use of the word 'despotism': 'The poverty of the French language restricts us to the use of words which, luckily, our government today rejects, with good reason. We hope that our enlightened readers will understand us and will not confuse absurd political despotism with the very prurient despotism of libertine passions' (p. 283). This extraordinarily subtle distinction tries to sort out the nearly inevitable confusion between a momentary, imaginary feeling of mastery and a formalization of that mastery into an enduring system. Fleeting possession (to return to the word at stake in our quotation from the pamphlet) need not be formalized into property rights ('far from *m'en formaliser*, I enjoy it').

Saint-Ange renders homage to Dolmancé, yet escapes formal feudal bondage by giving homage for *her* pleasure ('*I want* to be the victim of his error'), and not in exchange for protection. Irigaray is afraid of being trapped by her debt, but in her militant refusal she becomes a rigid virgin–phallicized. She believes there must be a way out of the Freudian/Lacanian Oedipal closed circuit, but revolt against the Father is no way out. Revolt against the Father, the violent refusal to honour and respect, *is* the Oedipal complex (Oedipus not recognizing his father, which kills the old man). Irigaray has simply switched from the female unresolved Oedipus to the male Oedipus. Which completes her *homm-age*, her becoming a man in relation to Lacan.

What to do? What would Saint-Ange do? She counsels her protegée on that very problem: 'If your father, who is a libertine, desires you, marvellous, let him use you for his pleasure [*qu'il jouisse de toi*], but without enslaving you' (p. 66). Let him take possession of you, let him have orgasm from you, but without subjugating you to his law.

7   Writing Erratic Desire

Irigaray's *Speculum de l'autre femme* (1974) was reviewed by another woman Lacanian analyst, Eugénie Luccioni, in the journal *Esprit* (March 1975). This review, full of praise for Irigaray's 'talent', regrets her taking the wrong direction–political/philosophical rather than psychoanalytic. A year later (1976) Eugénie Luccioni, now called Eugénie Lemoine-Luccioni (more on that name change later), published (in Lacan's series 'Le Champ freudien' at Éditions du Seuil) a book on women, *Partage des femmes*. In the introduction to that book Lemoine-Luccioni states that 'what is at stake here is an analytic effort and not a philosophical or a political one' (p. 11). There follows a footnote referring to Irigaray's book. Lemoine-Luccioni's book can thus be read as an effort in the right direction, the direction she feels Irigaray should have taken and regrettably did not. A year later (October 1977) Irigaray published an article in the journal *Critique* which is, among other things, a review of Lemoine-Luccioni's *Partage des femmes*. In this *Critique* article, 'Misère de la psychanalyse', Irigaray is positively vitriolic.

In this chapter I propose to follow some of the more eccentric contours of this 'quarrel' between Irigaray and Lemoine-Luccioni. Not in order to determine who is right in some univocal and personal way, but because this debate which centres on the subject of the relation of psychoanalysis to politics as it concerns women is a difficult and important question for the present book, for psychoanalysis, and for feminism. Among other things, evidence the fact, mentioned in the first chapter of our book, that one of the strongest continuing feminist theory groups in France is called 'Psychoanalysis and Politics'. Let us recall that that 'and'–like Juliet Mitchell's 'and' (*Psychoanalysis and Feminism*) which we echo in our title–is, despite its innocuous appearance, a very problematic word.

The gesture with which I begin my reading of Mitchell's book, the gesture of attending to the 'and', the gesture of paying attention to small details is not simply some external methodological device, but is the very stuff of what I am trying to advance as a psychoanalytic, feminist reading. Lacan would call it attention to the letter. Feminists might call it attention to context, to materiality, which refuses the imperialistic, idealizing reductions that have been solidary with a denigration of the feminine–material, localized, at home, *in situ*–in favour of the masculine–active, ideal, in movement, away from the home.

Irigaray and Lemoine-Luccioni both endorse such reading. Their differences are relatively small (hence most disquieting),[1] indeed both are Lacanian-trained women psychoanalysts interested in working on and writing about women. I hope in this chapter to avoid as much as possible the incredible temptation to polarize the differences between these two into an opposition. This problem of dealing with difference without constituting an opposition may just be what feminism is all about (might even be what psychoanalysis is all about). Difference produces great anxiety. Polarization, which is a theatrical representation of difference, tames and binds that anxiety. The classic example is sexual difference which is represented as a polar opposition (active–passive, energy–matter–all polar oppositions share the trait of taming the anxiety that specific differences provoke).[2]

Returning to the matter of a specific reading, one attentive to detail, in the introduction to *Partage des femmes* Lemoine-Luccioni writes: 'If analysis does not cling to that which is most particular [*particulier*, specific] in the subject's desire . . ., analysis will lose itself in a generalized science that precisely renders desire aseptic' (p. 11). Irigaray could not agree more. But she accuses Lemoine-Luccioni of merely 'using what is particular in the subject's desire as a *proof*' for the analyst's universal, for 'the Lacanian code, *a priori* and universal' ('Misère', p. 833). According to Irigaray, Lemoine-Luccioni is not really listening to the unknown of the patient's desire, but rather in any analysis she is finding what the Lacanian orthodoxy prepares her to find there. In 'Misère de la psychanalyse' Irigaray's quarrel is no longer with Freud or even with Lacan but with the 'orthodox' Lacanians. And it is no coincidence that her tone of self-righteous sarcasm and her accusations that institutionalized psychoanalytic dogma is used for mastery over analysands sound like Lacan's 1950s diatribes against the Freudian orthodoxy (Anna Freud and the ego psychologists).[3]

Irigaray considers Lemoine-Luccioni to be trapped in her wish to please Lacan, afraid to stray from Lacan's words, afraid to risk unauthorization by getting lost in a new encounter with some other unconscious, some other desire, rather than the recognizable, already 'known' Lacanian Unconscious, Lacanian Desire. Certainly Lemoine-Luccioni is more faithful to Lacan. Certainly she can be a member of his school and be published in his series, whereas Irigaray was ousted from a Lacanian Department of Psychoanalysis where she was teaching. But ironically it is Irigaray who is carrying on Lacan's most radical battle, the battle against the institutionalized stagnation of psychoanalysis. Such institutionalization domesticates the unconscious, 'renders desire aseptic', protects the analyst's prestige and power, and short-circuits the 'aim' of analysis which is to get the subject to assume her/his own desire.[4]

To the extent that Lacan is the 'Master' of a psychoanalytic institution, he cannot carry on that battle. To the extent that any disciple is inscribed by his or her fidelity to the master, this cannot be that disciple's battle. Yet the battle must go on, if psychoanalysis is to live and be vivifying. The similarity between Irigaray's 'Misère de la psychanalyse' and Lacan's 'La Chose freudienne' ('The Freudian Thing') is stunning. Irigaray, excommunicated by the Lacanian institution, is in the position Lacan occupied in the 1950s when he had been excluded from the International Psychoanalytic Association. She shares the strengths and weaknesses of that position. She can give a radical critique of the power structures of the psychoanalytic institution, but is also trapped within an unlucid anger, an ego-gratifying righteousness that is recognizable as a 'political' stance, and incompatible with the role of the psychoanalyst. Certainly what is borne out by Irigaray's repetition of Lacan's earlier position is Lacan's notion that it is position within an intersubjective network rather than some intrinsic personality that determines one's discourse and behaviour, and that any person might fill any position.[5] But what is also borne out is that analytic work, writing, theory is always political, always involved with power structures. Psychoanalysis invokes authority and to refuse to analyze psychoanalytic politics is not to be apolitical, but to shore up the master's power, institutional power, and to ensure the patients' submission to institutionalized discourse.

In her claim that Lemoine-Luccioni simply subjects the specificity of the subject's desire to the Lacanian universal, Irigaray asks: 'what kind of gesture can we suppose in this subjection of the analysand's language to a system of signifiers that is not his/hers?' She goes on to answer her own question in no uncertain terms: 'if there can be a "dictionary" or a "bible" of Freudian or Lacanian discourse, there can be neither "dictionary" nor "grammar" of psychoanalysis as such without risk of adapting the analysands to a language other than that which they speak. Interpretation, and simply listening, would thus come back to an act of mastery by the analyst over the analysand, to an instrument in the service of a master and *his* truth' ('Misère', p. 884).

Reading *Partage des femmes* one would protest this violent condemnation. The book is original, and full of attentiveness to the peculiar associative networks of certain 'cases', both patients and literary texts. Indeed Lemoine-Luccioni works out many of her concepts in terms derived from a particular case, a classic psychoanalytic procedure starting from Freud. Irigaray cites no specific sites of Lemoine-Luccioni's sacrificing the patient's specificity to the master's truth. But there are examples to be found. Their importance for our investigation is not their frequency but their nodal position.

One particular example seems fortuitously to take us to the densest heart of our questions about power, discourse, psychoanalysis and women: '"It is flabbergasting how much I can dream of a phallus not in its place" says a young woman shortly before giving birth (phallus for penis)' (*Partage*, p. 23). The corrective parenthesis–'(phallus for penis)'–is Lemoine-Luccioni's, and it is shocking.

The woman says 'phallus', but according to her analyst she 'means' penis. This implies that there is some fundamental discourse which the analyst 'knows', and with which the analysand is not yet sufficiently acquainted. Lemoine-Luccioni must act as her interpreter. The discourse of which Lemoine-Luccioni has greater mastery we presume to be Lacanian. A commonplace of Lacanian doctrine is the separation of the concepts 'phallus' and 'penis', which are confused in Freud's writings. Lacan's contribution to Freudian theory of sexual difference is to articulate the castration complex around the phallus, which is symbolic, the maternal phallus, to be understood by reference to Freud's phallic phase. The phallus, unlike the penis, is lacking to any subject, male or female. The phallus symbolizing unmediated, full *jouis-*

sance must be lacking for any subject to enter the symbolic order, that is to enter language, effective intersubjectivity. Human desire, according to Lacanian doctrine, is always mediated by signification. That is our human lot of castration. The ultimate Lacanian goal is for the subject 'to assume his/her castration'.

So, if the phallus is that which is always lacking, if any subject is always already castrated in order to be a subject, have a particularity of desire, be inscribed in language, in the human community, then this patient's dream 'of a phallus not in its place' is a more 'Lacanian dream' than Lemoine-Luccioni's correction of it. The Lacanian reference to the maternal phallus leads to the formulation that the phallus is that which is 'not in its place': Lemoine-Luccioni's patient dreams Lacanian theory.

Is that what the analyst must correct? The phallus, privileged signifier of the symbolic order, of Lacanian discourse, belongs to the analyst. The analysand is to talk of penises. It is no coincidence that the phallus is linked to power, by way of the notion of potency. The phallus is the attribute (always necessarily veiled) of the powerful (the presumedly omnipotent and omniscient phallic mother, the symbolic father, the King, the Other). Perhaps the word 'phallus' is also an attribute of power, belonging to the masters, the theoreticians, and not the analysands who should have only the word 'penis'.

This distinction between 'phallus' and 'penis' has everything to do with the question of psychoanalysis and politics, the debate acted out by Irigaray and Lemoine-Luccioni. Lacanians think feminist claims are based on a confusion of penis and phallus. And Lacanians would separate the two notions. There is no phallic inequity; that is, neither sex can be or have the phallus. Thus women have no reason to rail against the phallus's privilege. The inequities between men and women are based upon a general societal confusion between penis and phallus. The answer to this problem is not to alter the phallocentrism of discourse (a philosophical/political answer) but to separate the symbolic phallus from the penis (real or imaginary). Thus the problem (the confusion) can be resolved within the domain of psychoanalysis (therapy and theory).

Certainly the signifier 'phallus' functions in distinction from 'penis', but it must also always refer to 'penis'. Lacanians seem repeatedly to try to clear up that distinction as if it could be done once and for all. It would be satisfying to tame the anxiety produced by the small, specific, always contextual differences between 'phallus' and 'penis'. With that view, Lacanians would perhaps wish to polarize the two terms into an opposition. But that is hard to do with synonyms. Such attempts to remake language to one's own theoretical needs, as if language were merely a tool one could wield, is a very naive, un-Lacanian view of language

The question of whether one can separate 'phallus' from 'penis' rejoins the question of whether one can separate psychoanalysis from politics. The penis is what men have and women do not; the phallus is the attribute of power which neither men nor women have. But as long as the attribute of power is a phallus which refers to and can be confused (in the imaginary register?) with a penis, this confusion will support a structure in which it seems reasonable that men have power and women do not. And as long as psychoanalysts maintain the separability of 'phallus' from 'penis', they can hold on to their 'phallus' in the belief that their discourse has no relation to sexual inequality, no relation to politics.

One of the major stumbling blocks in the Lacanian notion of the phallus with its reference to Freud is that in Freud the woman's version of the castration complex is called 'penis envy'. As much as it seems smarter theory to say that what the woman 'really' wants is not the penis but the phallus, Freud uses the word 'penis' in his formulation. Here is Lemoine-Luccioni's articulation of phallus and penis-envy: 'When by chance, [the girl] was given the opportunity to see a penis, the desire for the phallus was translated by penis envy' (*Partage*, p. 70). 'Penis envy' is a 'translation' of 'desire for the phallus'. One language, accidentally, 'by chance', provides us with a translation, a secondary form of an original. 'Penis envy' is Freud's term; 'phallus' and 'desire' are two privileged Lacanian terms. Yet 'penis envy 'seems to be secondary, accidental, a translation of the more originary Lacanian formulation.

Irigaray's suspicion is that Lacanian discourse functions as some fundamental referent which any analysand's discourse can only 'translate', approximate to in some secondary, inadequate way (thus necessitating Lemoine-Luccioni's work as interpreter in her corrective parenthesis–'phallus for penis'). This suspicion is borne out by a statement in a book by the exemplarily loyal Lacanian Serge Leclaire (*On tue un enfant* 1975). Leclaire's style in this book resembles that of *Partage des femmes*, and there are somewhat obscure but very sympathetic references to each other's work in these two books (published a year apart in Lacan's series at Seuil). Leclaire writes: 'the phallus, *referent* of the unconscious order, cannot be grasped in a concept:. . . it escapes. . . all inscription. That is to say that there exists neither image nor text of the phallus' (pp. 32–3, my italics). Any image or text is but a 'translation' of the phallus which is no longer a signifier, not even the privileged signifier, but a referent, that which language always invokes, always indicates, but which always exceeds it. Now certainly when Lacan talks about the 'castration' entailed by the subject's being in language, in the symbolic order, a good way to understand it is that one is always deprived of signifying the referent, one's language is doomed to never being more than a good translation. But to say that 'phallus', a signifier forming part of our language, is the name of that unreachable, unspeakable referent constitutes 'phallus' as some fundamental, transcendental truth.

Lemoine-Luccioni writes: 'If by chance the girl catches sight of a penis–a fact in itself contingent–this latter becomes the sign of the phallus' (*Partage*, p. 45). The penis, through the contingencies of experience, can become the sign of the phallus–sign as opposed to referent–can stand for the phallus. But the 'phallus' does not depend on any contingencies; it is originary, essential, transcendental. Yet 'phallus', the signifier in its specificity, in its letter not its spirit–which is how any Lacanian ought to take a signifier–is always a reference to 'penis'. 'Phallus' cannot function as signifier in ignorance of 'penis'. 'Phallus' is not the originary, proper name of some referent that may get contingently translated as 'penis'. 'Phallus' confronts the inadequacy of any name to embody the referent, and is itself emblematic of that inadequacy by its necessary dependence on 'penis', the necessary inclusion of 'penis' in any definition of 'phallus'.

One of the weaknesses of the Lacanian orthodoxy is to render 'phallus' transcendental, an originary name, not dependent on 'penis' and its contingencies. Yet that is not, I would say, the status of the signification of the phallus at its most interesting in Lacan's work. Lacan, indeed, tries to rectify this transcendental, metalinguistic notion of the phallus in his reading of Ernest Jones's 'Theory of Symbolism'. Lacan refers to Jones's 'remark, *fallacious* in fascinating by its reference to the object, that if the church tower can symbolize the phallus, never will the phallus symbolize the tower' (my italics).[6] Jones would make the phallus a final referent, one that does not symbolize anything else but is the thing itself, self-referential. Lacan considers such a view of the phallus fallacious.

The word 'fallacious' likewise crops up in Lemoine-Luccioni's discussion of the phallus. For example: 'This problematic of theft responds to what the woman would lack and which she would be deprived of and to the *fallacious* gift she awaits from the father' (*Partage*, p. 59, my italics). Elsewhere in Lemoine-Luccioni and in Freud, it is said that the gift the daughter awaits from the father is the phallus—in the form of a penis (her penis, his penis), or a baby—but the gift is phallic, making up for her 'lack' which is a phallic lack. The 'phallic' gift becomes a 'fallacious' gift. There is some insistent link between phallic reasoning, theories of the phallus, and fallacious reasoning. Somehow to try to think the phallus is to wind up with fallacy.

Irigaray asks in her accusation: 'your often contradictory and embroiled statements on the status of the phallus in relation to the real organ or the real sex, do they not have also as their cause . . . to maintain veiled from your gaze and that of others how it stands with the sex organ of your Father in psychoanalysis' ('Misère', p. 886). The analysts do not want to clear up, to reveal the status of the phallus. According to Lacan, the phallus 'can play its role only when veiled'.[7] To clear all this up is to reveal/ unveil the Father's 'Phallus' as a mere 'penis', as one signifier among others, prey to the contingencies of the letter, of the materiality of signification, alienated from the referent. Lacanian analysts protect Lacanian discourse from being just another 'contingent translation'. The stake is the Father's Phallus. To confuse and thus veil the status of the father's 'phallus' is to endow him with a 'Phallus' which he then might give to any daughter, to any analyst.

The daughter, in this case Lemoine-Luccioni, awaits the phallic gift, the fallacious gift. In the sentence quoted earlier she writes: 'When by chance, [the girl] was given the opportunity to see a penis, the desire for the phallus was translated by penis envy' (*Partage*, p. 70). The girl, 'by chance', if she is lucky, is 'given the opportunity to see a penis'. That opportunity, that sight, is a 'gift', something wondrous, a wonder for the girl. For Lemoine-Luccioni, for the analyst, for the daughter, the privilege of the phallus is linked to the wonder of the penis. 'The *phallic* function is specifically that which also causes the penis *to become erect*. Then it becomes soft again: it falls. These are not metaphors. How is it that this spectacular penis, thus erected, does not ordinarily become an object of pleasure for itself, but is the instrument of sexual *jouissance*? And that it finds in penetration of another body its pleasure?' (*Partage*, p. 168).

The penis is 'spectacular'. Yet what is most wonderful to Lemoine-Luccioni is that this 'spectacular' erection is not an end in itself, is not self-referential, self-sufficient, is not 'an object of pleasure for itself'. What she cannot believe is that this phallic penis (a pleonasm, to be sure) is an instrument; she can barely believe that it wants 'another body', needs another body for its pleasure, its fulfilment. The erect penis, contrary to the symbolic veiled phallus, is not monolithic power, but desire, need for another body. Lemoine-Luccioni finds it hard to believe that the erect penis is not an end in and for itself, because the phallus, the Lacanian Phallus, is just that, the attribute of she or he that is whole, not needy of the other.

Obviously such a phallus cannot be or be had by anyone. Yet the difficulty in believing that the erect penis is not in- and for-itself is a symptom of the inevitable confusion between penis and phallus. And rather than see the phallus as a penis, Lemoine-Luccioni prefers to see the penis as a phallus. 'These are not metaphors', she writes. When one talks of the 'penis'—not even the 'phallus' here but the very contingent penis with its ups and downs—one is no longer dealing with a slippery, always metaphorical language. A metaphor is one signifier in the place of another signifier. In a Lacanian view of language a signifier always signifies another signifier; no word is free from metaphoricity. The speaking subject cannot control whether his/her words are metaphors. Lemoine-Luccioni would believe that in speaking of the wondrous, spectacular penis, one is finally speaking of the referent, of the thing itself.

(There is something suspect, uncomfortable about my trying to regulate Lemoine-Luccioni's words according to 'a Lacanian view of language'. Am I not simply doing what Irigaray accuses Lemoine-Luccioni of doing? Am I not reducing the specificity of this woman's book by wanting to bring it back into the domain of Lacanian discourse?)

I would like to read Lemoine-Luccioni's marvel at the penis as more than a mistake to be corrected. I do not want to write, as she did, a rectifying parenthesis–(penis for phallus). I would like to read this passage in cognizance of it as exciting, excited, erotic. Speaking *within* the confusion between penis and phallus, she is speaking her desire. The two questions at the end of the passage are the mark of something that goes far beyond what Irigaray has criticized as her filial fidelity to Lacan. Those questions bespeak a desire for the penis not the Paternal (or Maternal) Phallus. A desire that barely dares believe that there is a penis, that barely can see beyond the Phallus. But if there were a penis. . . One that could desire to penetrate another body, one that could want a woman, need a woman, not just a 'woman', but more excitingly an 'other' body, not woman as the appropriate phallic object, but an 'other body'. . .

The trouble with Irigaray's polemical stance, political position, is that it forces her to hear only the Law, not the desire in *Partage des femmes*. From that position, Irigaray cannot listen to the erratic, erotic letter of Lemoine-Luccioni's book. Irigaray's adversary position traps her into repeating the fault of which she accuses the other woman–not listening to the '*particulier* of the subject's desire', but only using it as 'proof' for an argument. Irigaray's text is abundant with quotations from Lemoine-Luccioni, but they only serve to illustrate Irigaray's argument.

Is this division between a 'political' reading and a 'psychoanalytic' reading inevitable? Must one either read for position or read for specificity? I think this division not totally inescapable. Obviously the worst tendency, the inherent constitutional weakness of psychoanalysis, is to be apolitical (which is to say, to support the institutions in power) and the worst tendency in political positions is to obliterate desire and specificity. But there are moments in the work of both Irigaray and Lemoine-Luccioni (among others) which are neither or both or something slightly other.

These momentary possibilities are inevitably left behind in a return to polar oppositions (political versus psychoanalytic, for example). But the fact that both women attain to such moments, are able, even ever so briefly, to inscribe a certain desire in the exposition of a theoretical position, bespeaks the project they both share: to pursue a practice, both of psychoanalysis and of writing, that attends to the specificity of the subject's desire.

Irigaray delineates two modes of reading the unconscious:

'Either the unconscious is nothing but what has already been heard by you... or the unconscious is desire which attempts to speak itself and, as analysts, you have to listen without excluding. However much this listening to everything might bring about callings into question of *your* desire... Whatever the risk of *your* death that might ensue' ('Misère', p. 881). Clinging to the specificity of the other's discourse involves the risk of loss of identity, loss of self, alienation, death. Analysis, if it is not to be a process of adapting the patient to some reigning order of discourse, must include the risk of unseating the analyst. No one can be master of the unconscious, even those whose profession it is to seek it out.

Irigaray complains that Lemoine-Luccioni does not expose her desire, her fantasies, her transference, in other words the effects of her unconscious. Elsewhere Irigaray writes: 'If I wrote up a case history... I would not do it as it has always been done: by the "report", the dissection, the interpretation of only the analysand's transference, but by restaging *both* transferences.'[8] This seems to be what she regrets Lemoine-Luccioni is not doing, not staging her own transference. Irigaray calls for a new sort of psychoanalytic writing, one in which the analyst's mastery is undercut by the recognition that the analyst too has an unconscious which traverses the analytic scene. She admits that 'the question, technically, is certainly not easy' ('Misère', p. 889). The technique of mastery—one unconscious (the patient's) and one neutral, scientific interpreter/reporter (the analyst)—is 'easier'. Such case-histories remain within the classical discourse of science, with its separation between subject and object. A case-history cognizant of the analyst–narrator's desire must proceed through uncharted paths.

Lemoine-Luccioni *does not* give an account of her transference, it is true. But *perhaps* she *does more*. The analyst–narrator's desire does not just traverse the analytic scene, it acts out in the scene of writing.[9] Lemoine–Luccioni's transference is not narrated, mediated, tamed, explained and re-presented. It is present in the text, acting out in the most disconcerting way. Irigaray's imagined account of her own transference might still, after all, enhance her position, for such a gesture would be coherent with her theory. She would be in the correct 'feminist', revolutionary, non-masterful position. Yet being in the correct position is self-mastery, self-possession. Something more uncanny seems to occur in *Partage des femmes*—something that leaves the reader wondering who the author is, where she is, what she intends. In other words (and perhaps the gesture of 'in other words' is always a return of the unknown to the already known), the reader encounters the analyst–narrator–writer's unconscious.

(In all this talk of correct narrative position, staging one's own transference, risking one's identity, I begin to feel less and less sure of what might be the 'correct position' for me, of whether I, like Irigaray, am trying to regain self-mastery by the best ruse of all. Of course that may be the goal of psychoanalysis: greater self-possession not through rigidity but through more resiliency, more openness to the effects of one's unconscious. A few pages back I found myself switching sides, from Irigaray's side to Lemoine-Luccioni's. That was momentarily disconcerting. But then I began to find it gratifying. I reflected that my avowed project in this chapter—and in this book—is to avoid getting locked into a specular opposition, and that a blatant switch was perhaps a good way to practise such avoidance, since taking sides seems inevitable in any attempt to be engaged as a reader, or to engage my reader.

But then, this parenthesis itself seems at once the most and the least unsettling gesture of all. It is a last-ditch attempt to regain the correct position, the correct position here being to be unsettled from any position. The real risk avoided here is the risk of being wrong.)

The letter of Lemoine-Luccioni's text is really quite odd, quite singular. *Partage des femmes* contains a few glaring, outrageous errors. Our reading of the 'Freudian slips' in this book is invited by the author. On the second page of the text she writes: 'Woman is the truth that [man] interrogates in order to make holes in [*trouer*] the secret of creation (and I am willingly keeping the typographical error: *trouer* [to make holes in] in place of *trouver* [to find]).' She meant to write 'in order to find the secret of creation'. By leaving out just one letter, she writes instead, 'in order to make holes in the secret of creation'. Obviously such slips, like most effects of the unconscious, are awkward to translate: another reminder that Freud's discoveries are in language, not metalinguistic or transcendental. Lemoine-Luccioni chooses to keep her 'typo', to expose it to the reader. The effect of that choice goes beyond what any author can control. At each instance of the word 'trouer' or the word 'trouver' throughout the book (and there are many), we attempt to substitute the other one. Our reading is very much directed by this early exhibited slip. What we find (*trouver*) as readers has the effect of making holes in (*trouer*) the work.

Lemoine-Luccioni's blatant errors concern names, either author's names or book titles. Twice (p. 11 and p. 64) she footnotes Irigaray's book, the book she 'herself' reviewed (or not quite 'herself') since it was Eugénie Luccioni who signed the review (another case of altering a name?). But she gives the title of Irigaray's books as *Le Speculum de l'autre femme* (adding a definite article to the beginning). Is this slip simply to be understood as an act of aggression against her adversary? Should we not link it to the risk of loss of identity incurred by any encounter with the unconscious?

In the second footnote to Irigaray (p. 64) Lemoine-Luccioni makes another mistake. She refers to an article of Irigaray's as 'The Blind Spot in [*dans*] an Old Dream of Symmetry', whereas the correct title is 'The Blind Spot of [*de*] an Old Dream of Symmetry'. This same footnote which makes two mistakes in Irigaray's titles includes the information that there is a review of *Le Speculum de l'autre femme* (*sic*) by Eugénie Luccioni in *Esprit*, March 1975. It is always somewhat strange to write or read a footnote to a text by the author of the work in which the footnote appears. A writer must decide whether to put the footnote in the first or third person, whether to refer to 'my text' or use one's own name as if it were another person's. In this case the oddness of the situation is underlined by the use of a name which differs from the author's name. Eugénie Luccioni is presumably 'the same person' as Eugénie Lemoine-Luccioni, but the discrepancy makes one aware of the name and its conventional relation to identity.

All this becomes more curious when reinserted into the network of various other footnotes in *Partage des femmes*. Page 104: a footnote to an article by Gennie Luccioni in the same journal *Esprit*, April 1959. Page 115: a footnote to a book by Gennie and Paul Lemoine, 1972. Page 119: a footnote to a seminar contribution by Paul Lemoine, 1974. One assumes that Paul Lemoine is the author's husband, and that Gennie/Eugénie is the author. Page 137: a footnote to an article by G. Luccioni, *Esprit*, December 1967. The 'G.' presumably stands for Gennie; still it is striking that each work of the author footnoted in this book has a different signature. Finally on page 147, one reaches the limit-case—a footnote to a book by Maartje Luccioni. This is presumably *not* the author. But the relationship is still troubling: the last name is the same; is it a relative? The title of the book is in an unidentified foreign language–*Voie nugeen huis heaft*–but no publisher or publication date is given, as is the usual practice in this book's references. Besides, the footnote continues to say (with a certain allusion of intimacy) that the quotation from this book given in the text is 'an extemporaneous translation by the novelist, which I kept so as to conserve the raw tone'. One almost suspects that the foreign novel and this 'Maartje' are made up. The limits to the author's identity, as it relates to these references beyond the text itself, are strained.

All this play with the identity of an author in the margins of *Partage des femmes* echoes something Lemoine-Luccioni says in the text, in the chapter called 'The Brother and the Sister'. She has been describing a certain relation between brother and sister based on the fiction that they are twins: if they were twins, the only difference between them would be one of sexual opposition. Yet in the cases she studies the siblings are not actually twins, but have an age difference that is being suppressed by their family myth. The refusal of such specific differences serves to constitute a polar opposition rather than a confrontation with differences. Lemoine-Luccioni writes: 'Besides it is not true that they have the same origin. Born at different moments, they are born of different parents. But they want their parents, like essences, to be immutable' (p. 113).

Like children, the various productions of an author date from different moments, and cannot strictly be considered to have the same origin, the same author. At least we must avoid the fiction that a person is the same, unchanging throughout time. Lemoine-Luccioni makes the difficulty patent by signing each text with a different name, all of which are 'hers'. Since the various names are not totally different, are not pseudonyms, one can presume to recognize what one commonly calls 'the same person', but one is forced to note some difficulty, a certain trembling at the edges of that identity.

The choice of the double name 'Lemoine-Luccioni' for the author of *Partage des femmes* seems particularly enlightening. Lemoine is apparently the husband's name; Luccioni her professional name, still used in articles that postdate the joint work by Gennie and Paul Lemoine. The hyphenated name makes the author a double creature. The thesis of *Partage des femmes* is that it is woman's lot [*partage*] in our social arrangements to bear an internal division [*partage.*] The division between men and women is lived as a division within woman. The double name Lemoine-Luccioni gives the author a double identity which repeats the doubleness of man and wife. The woman's usual assumption of the man's name in marriage gives them the same name, a unity of identity. The choice of a hyphenated name continues to assert the difference between the two spouses. But in general, it is only the wife who bears the hyphenated name, bears the division. The husband retains his unified name. One could say that the identity, the name, of the author of *Partage des femmes* is not external to the book, but is created with the book, as part of the book.

Speaking of the moment of giving birth and the loss it entails for the mother, Lemoine-Luccioni writes: 'in that instant, the woman no longer *has* it and she *is* nothing' (pp. 53–4). Much of this book speaks of the phallic fulfilment of pregnancy and of the castratory loss in parturition (another *partage*, division of the woman). At this moment Lemoine-Luccioni articulates that loss doubly, as a loss in having ('*has* it no longer') and a loss in being ('*is* nothing'). If we return to the analogy constructed earlier between a book and a child, then the double loss involved in giving birth to a book would affect the book (which the author 'has no longer') and the author/parent's very identity ('is nothing'). The sentence immediately preceding this one we have just quoted about having and being nothing reads: 'It is a patent failure which exposes her to "a mutilation. . . which will be inscribed in being along the lines of fragilization of the fragmented body" as Granoff and Périer write in their "Research on Femininity".' There is a 'patent failure', a blatant error in this sentence itself, two actually. First, the second author's name is spelled 'Perrier', not 'Périer'. Second, the title of the Granoff and Perrier article is 'The Problem of Perversion in Woman and Feminine Ideals', not 'Research on Femininity'. By her slips, Lemoine-Luccioni has deprived an author of his production (child) as well as his name (self, whole unto itself, phallicly self-referential).

The two mistakes on page 53, in their specificity, provide certain associations. In misspelling Perrier's name, Lemoine-Luccioni leaves an 'r' out. A few pages later (indeed on the same page where we find the double error in Irigaray's titles, p. 64), she writes: 'One must not understand too fast, says J. Lacan. There is no big risk. But the warning functions mainly as a declaration of principle. To whomever believes s/he understands right away and completely, one can affirm that s/he is mistaken, if only from the simple fact that meaning is not fixed.... It is appropriate to allow a floating course [*une "erre" de flottement*].' The floating course is the 'appropriate' tack, the 'correct position', for one who wants to avoid a 'position', that is, to avoid a stance, a stationing which by being 'fixed', must be 'mistaken'. The word she uses and even puts into quotation marks is a 'warning' not to 'understand too fast', a signal not to proceed so quickly by, but to attend to the specificity of the word. The word 'erre' is pronounced exactly like the letter 'r' in French. So to 'allow a floating course' might also be read as 'to leave an "r" floating', which is what she does to Perrier's name.

The quotation marks around 'erre' not only alert the reader to the sound of the word, but also send her running to the dictionary. 'Erre' has an archaic meaning as 'manner of proceeding, of walking' and a nautical meaning of 'speed gained by a ship which is no longer driven by the propeller'.[10] So an 'erre de flottement' is a pleonasm, the term 'erre' already implies floating. 'Erre' also reminds us of 'erreur' (error). Lemoine-Luccioni finds it appropriate to allow an *erre* so as to avoid an *erreur*.

The dictionary tells us that 'erre' (the noun) is derived from the Old French 'errer'. One would think that this is the word which gives us 'error' and 'err', but to think that one would be in error. Apparently there were two different words 'errer' in Old French: one derives from the Latin *iterare* (to travel), the other from the Latin *errare* (which this dictionary fails to translate). In modern French too, there are two meanings of 'errer': the first, archaic or literary, means 'to be mistaken'; the modern, common meaning is 'to wander'. But we are told (parenthetically) that the modern, common meaning is the result of 'confusion of the [first meaning] with the old French word *errer* "to travel"'. If our reader is now confused by our wanderings, she can consider herself in good company. Apparently, an entire linguistic people were no less confused. As the result of this confusion, the meaning strayed, (dare we say it), wandered, from 'to be mistaken', this wandering being the result of a general 'error'. Lemoine-Luccioni is not the only one who seems led by 'erre' into pleonasm.

Yet what is this error of the francophones, denounced by the dictionary's corrective parenthesis (reminiscent of Lemoine-

Luccioni's 'phallus for penis')? The word 'errer' derived from *errare* originally meant 'to be mistaken', and through general error strayed from that meaning so it came to mean 'to wander'. Yet a Latin dictionary[11] informs us that 'errare' properly means 'to wander' and figuratively means 'to wander from the truth, to err'. So that all the confusion in Old French produced an error which caused 'errer' to wander back to the proper meaning of 'errare'.

All this is reminiscent of the title of Lacan's 1973–4 Seminar: 'Les non-dupes errent' (The non-dupes wander/err). That fact (Lacan's seminar title) reassures me that I may still be on the right course with all this wandering. But my foray into the dictionary, induced by Lemoine-Luccioni's 'erre de flottement', has led me (unwittingly?) into an unwieldy digression which I fear is not 'appropriate' to this book, to my aim. The question may be: is my 'floating' a 'manner of progressing' (archaic sense of 'erre') or an error? That I should have allowed such a floating seems both nice and disturbing. Nice: an appropriate sort of acting out, giving proof of engagement in my subject, of a willingness to let go control and be moved by textual currents. Disturbing: first, because it does not seem 'important to the book' to spend so much time on scholarly etymology, so much time on one word; and secondly, because it is all too 'appropriate', all too nice, all too Lacanian, all too predictable. I am not sure there is a difference between the first and second reason for my disturbance. I am sure that this reflection on my feelings about the digression is very similar to the earlier parenthesis about what my 'correct position' should be. Finally (?) I wonder if these self-reflections are not facile and self-indulgent, narcissistic, exhibitionistic and modish. And then I wonder if the previous sentence (and paragraph) is not just a rationalization for my resistance to exposing my uncertainties.

My trip into the dictionary seems to have induced certain repetitions, certain acting outs. It seems appropriate to say that I have had a transference onto the dictionary. Now this is neither so silly nor so precious as it might sound. According to Lacan, transference occurs in a relation to a 'subject presumed to know'. In transference one considers the other as the Other (capital O). The Other means what s/he says and does what s/he means. The Other's language is not alienated and the Other knows what the subject's own discourse means. At one point, Lacan calls the Other, 'the locus of the signifier's treasure' (*Écrits*, p. 806;

Sheridan, p. 304). The gesture by which we go to the dictionary, the gesture of trying to find out what a mysterious word 'means', is the attempt to go to the place of the signifier's treasure. (In this vein, compare 'thesaurus', etymologically meaning 'treasure'.) The dictionary can function as the Other, and in that way, it is not surprising that it produces certain effects of transference.

I said above that *both* errors around Granoff and Perrier's article lead to useful associations. For a few pages we have been following the traces ('erres', the plural form of 'erre' means 'the traces of an animal'–the dictionary *does* seem to 'know'), the traces of Lemoine-Luccioni's floating 'r'. We will now go back to the second mistake, the title of the article. 'Research on Femininity' is not the title of the Granoff and Perrier article, but it *is* the title of an article by Michèle Montrelay, to which Lemoine-Luccioni makes several other (correct) references in this same book. In Montrelay's book *L'Ombre et le nom* ('The Shadow and the Name'), where 'Research on Femininity' has been reprinted, there is a footnote to *Partage des femmes* which makes implicit reference to the problematic of the author's name we have been following here. In the chapter 'The Shadow', of the book *The Shadow and the Name* (a book which has no chapter called 'The Name'), the reader finds a footnote which includes the name of Lemoine-Luccioni's book (*Partage des femmes*) and the name of the book's author.[12] Except that Montrelay makes a 'mistake' about the author's name. She refers to *Partage des femmes* as the work of 'Gennie Lemoine'. A strange kind of mistake, not exactly a slip, but a misreading, a refusal to read what is written on the page based upon the presumption that Montrelay already 'knows' the author of the book.

Perhaps this misreading is in some way called for by *Partage des femmes*. Gennie Lemoine is the name used in 1972 for a joint project with her husband. That 1972 book, *Le Psychodrame*, can in our analogy be considered a child of their marriage. A reader of *Partage des femmes* can hardly avoid noticing the privilege afforded marriage and childbirth. The book unfortunately lends itself to being considered a conservative plea for women to find their fulfilment in normal heterosexual marriage and mother-hood–in other words, in the traditional lot (*partage*) of women. This is the book that should be signed Gennie Lemoine, and probably the book Montrelay reads. But the book signed Eugénie Lemoine-Luccioni is more than that. It is written by a split author, whose identity is not whole, but is traversed by a hyphen. That hyphen can be read as the Lacanian bar that afflicts the speaking subject, splits the subject, divides the signifier from the signified. It can also be read as a minus sign, the sign of a lack, a castration.[13] The two terms are not added, forming a union, but are subtracted. Neither the marriage (Lemoine and Luccioni), nor the married woman (Lemoine-Luccioni) are whole, unified, but are inhabited by a subtraction, a violence to union.

Yet *Partage des femmes* is not always up to the risk of assuming that hyphen. In a sense, it asks for Montrelay's 'misreading', for in so many weak moments it falls back into being the child of the good wife, Gennie Lemoine. For example:

> To write love, that then is the path of sublimation, the path which saves woman from nymphomania and erotomania. We do not concern ourselves with the natural path, in which, wife and mother, she comes to blossom: a path more difficult to encompass and disengage. But we do not deny it [the natural path]; we think it takes on all its meaning from the extreme paths represented by pathology on the one hand and sublimation on the other. (p. 93)

'Writing love', writing one's transference, acting out in the scene of writing is 'sublimation'. Certainly sublimation is better than pathology; but it seems inferior to 'the natural path in which [woman] comes to blossom'. There is here an ideal of the wife and mother, a natural fulfilment for woman. This would not be an 'extreme path', yet in its ideality, its naturalness, it is the most difficult to attain. Perhaps this is true. Surely Freud showed that the path to normal heterosexual femininity is so narrow and riddled with obstacles that attainment of its end—mature femininity—seems a near impossibility.

It seems Lemoine-Luccioni is writing in the context of the near impossibility of the natural path, and in that context still refusing to deny it—near impossible but *not* impossible. In fact *Partage des femmes* posits psychoanalysis as that which might help women reach 'the natural path', become fulfilled, healthy wives and mothers. That is what seems dangerously conservative, even reactionary about this book: these moments when successful marriage and motherhood take on an ideal glow. That is the book that might have been written by 'Gennie Lemoine', read by Michèle Montrelay.

But 'we do not concern ourselves with the natural path'. Although this book is in a large part about pregnancy, although it is based on her analyses of pregnant women, that is not where 'we' are concerned, are involved. That is not the scene of writing where the author's desire is staged. Eugénie Lemoine-Luccioni is engaged and inscribed in the project of 'writing love'. Her slips, errors about names, are all concerned with writing. It is there that one finds the book's unconscious, there that one finds the attempt of a desire to speak itself.

Perhaps the thematic content of the book—the subject of marriage and motherhood—serves most of all to disguise the investment in writing. Eugénie Lemoine-Luccioni is divided (*partagée*); she cannot wholly come to assume the place of 'writing love'. That path, which she calls sublimation, is where woman must be 'saved from nymphomania and erotomania'. Perhaps that is what frightens this good wife and mother. The confrontation with the necessity of being saved from such pathology is the confrontation with the very real risks of 'nymphomania and erotomania' she is running. To assume the place of her sublimation, the necessity of her sublimation, is to run the risk of her own 'pathology'.

The necessity of distancing herself from 'the pathological' may influence her suppression of the title of the Granoff and Perrier article: 'The Problem of Perversion in Woman and Feminine Ideals'. The reading of the paragraph we are now involved in certainly delineates some struggle both with perversion and with 'feminine ideals'—whether that last term relates to 'sublimation' or to 'the natural path'. There is also something archaic about the pathological terms 'nymphomania and erotomania'. That archaicism serves to distance those words from the scene of writing. These are not psychoanalytic terms, not Lacanian terms, but the terms of classical psychiatry with its presumptions of clear distinctions between the healthy doctors and the sick patients. In order for the author to give up her disguise as Gennie Lemoine, in order to avoid Montrelay's misreading, she would have to relinquish the models of pathology, and run the risks of her erratic, unnatural desire.

There is nothing 'natural', psychoanalysis seems to have discovered, about 'the natural path'. Nothing about it that is more 'natural' than writing or erotomania, except that it responds to woman's anatomical construction. But the detail of Lemoine-Luccioni's analyses shows again and again both the sublimation and the pathology that are mixed in with any act of giving birth.

Once the mother is a 'speaking subject', capable of sublimation or pathology, capable of writing love and losing her good name in wanton desire, there is more involved than anatomy, there is no longer any 'natural childbirth' possible.

This is certainly what Lemoine-Luccioni must mean when she considers 'the natural path' as being constituted by the extreme paths and as being the more difficult path. But still there remains a note of privilege to 'the natural' and a negative note to sublimation. We would prefer the implications of Michèle Montrelay's use of the term sublimation. She wishes to avoid the 'misinterpretation' of 'sublimation' that 'consists in seeing in it a passage from the sexual to the non-sexual' (*L'Ombre et le nom*, p. 74). Rather 'sublimation' involves giving up an infantile, unmediated relation to *jouissance* and operating in the register of metaphor and mediation, operating effectively in an adult order. 'Writing love' is certainly an instance of 'sublimation', but so is successful adult motherhood, even adult orgasm.

According to Montrelay there is no 'natural path' that leads directly from precocious, feminine, concentric sexuality (as discovered by Jones and the English School) to adult femininity. Without the detours of representation, metaphor, sublimation, even genital sexuality will always remain infantile. Lemoine-Luccioni finds that the greatest difficulty in mothering is the recognition of the separateness of the child (for example, see p. 49). As long as a mother remains in 'the natural path', that is, gives birth within an infantile, concentric, immediate economy, she will be unable to accept the necessity for a mediated, distanced relation to the child, for she will never have accepted such a 'sublimated', mediated relation to her mother. Writing is an exemplary instance of mediated communion, communication that recognizes distance. The detour of 'sublimation', of some sort of 'writing love', is necessary for the very kind of healthy mothering Lemoine-Luccioni poses as natural.

8 The Phallic Mother: Fraudian Analysis

The last essay in Irigaray's *Ce Sexe qui n'en est pas un* is a lyrical affirmation of a new, free love between women. That essay, 'Quand nos lèvres se parlent' (When our lips speak to each other), begins: 'If we continue to speak the same language to each other, we are going to reproduce the same history.' That text attempts not to repeat the same, rather to change, to make progress. But a parenthesis interrupts the lyrical flow, brusquely reminding the reader of a less idyllic, more familiar context: 'I love you, you who are neither mother (Excuse me Mother, I prefer a woman to you) nor sister' (p. 208). The need for excuses, the guilt of preferences seems to belong to another world, an ugly, awkward world which resents and resists change as infidelity. The parenthesis marks the intrusion of 'the same language', the language of obligation and familialism, from which this text would try to free 'us'.

To speak 'the same language' is to speak the *langue maternelle,* the mother tongue, taught the daughter by her mother. Irigaray does not want to 'reproduce the same history', and 'reproduce' is the mother's domain. No wonder then that the parenthetical throw-back is addressed to the mother. The obligation to reproduce—the daughter's obligation to reproduce the mother, the mother's story—is a more difficult obstacle than even the Father's Law, an obstacle that necessarily intrudes even into the lovely, liberated space of women among themselves.

After it calls into question the affirmative achievement at the end of *Ce Sexe*, this parenthesis then expands to become Irigaray's next 'book', *Et l'une ne bouge pas sans l'autre* (1979). That sixteen-page text is, like the parenthesis, addressed to Mother ('ma mère'). At once an expression of resentment at her mother's paralytic hold on her and an announcement of her leaving that bind, this little book makes it clear that the awkward, confused relation to the mother that momentarily intrudes into

113

the lyrical fantasy of a new love between women is no minor, marginal problem.

Et l'une ne bouge pas sans l'autre begins and ends with a statement of the paralysis her mother has given her. The book ends and still is not completed, not a 'book', a product, a separated achievement. Lacking the necessary volume to be a book, these sixteen spare pages have no right to stand on their own. The title means 'And one cannot move without the other'. Not only does the title evoke paralysis and the impossibility of separation, but the initial 'Et' conjoins it, in its very identity, to something prior. From the first word of its title this 'book' undermines its own claims to a separate existence. Yet it is published, in the world, the occasion for a daughter to represent the dilemma of her minority.

The speaker in *Et l'une*. . . pleads with her mother: 'You put yourself in my mouth, and I suffocate. . . . Continue to be also outside. Keep yourself/me also outside. Don't be engulfed, don't engulf me, in what passes from you to me. I would so much like that we both be here. That the one does not disappear into the other or the other into the one' (pp. 9 – 10). In *Speculum* Irigaray has written of an analogous engulfment in Freudian theory: 'thus "femininity" is effaced to leave room for maternity, is reabsorbed into maternity' (p. 88). What is the relation between the theoretical occulting of femininity by maternity and the engulfment of the daughter by her mother? Is it that Freud/man/theory can assimilate the otherness of woman into Mother (the complement to man's primary narcissism) thanks to a structural weakness in the distinction between a girl and her mother?[1]

In her very plea for separateness, its impossibility manifests itself. The oral relation ought to be one in which the daughter absorbs (from) the mother. Yet that transaction is confused with the mother's absorbing the daughter, since the difference between the two is not stable and since absorption is precisely a process which undermines boundary distinctions. Her pleas and formulations have a compulsive symmetry–'the one into the other or the other into the one'. Everything that happens to the one happens to the other. The only difference is that the daughter pleads with the mother as if it were in the mother's power (and not the daughter's) to change all this. The daughter can only plead, and the mother resist. Despite the constant claim of reabsorption, lack of solid differentiation, in this text the mother is always the 'you', and the daughter always the 'me'. The distinction of second and first person pronouns gives the daughter whatever fragile separateness she has. As long as she speaks there is a distinction.

Does this not lock the mother into the classic role of receiver of the child's discourse? The plea to the mother presumes the mother has the power to understand and fulfil the demand. Thus lack of satisfaction, lack of progress, lack of change to the unbearable situation which Irigaray bemoans, can only be understood as the mother's refusal to do what she is none the less empowered to do. When the daughter begs 'Keep yourself/me also outside', the statement supposes that the mother controls the process of absorption, of differentiation and identity. In Lacanian terms, the silent interlocutor, the second person who never assumes the first person pronoun, is the subject presumed to know, the object of transference, the phallic Mother, in command of the mysterious processes of life, death, meaning and identity. Locked into a transference, albeit a negative one, the speaker in *Et l'une. . .* is paralyzed in an eternal minority.

What if Irigaray were to let go of the rigid, fragile, arbitrary distinction between me and you, daughter and mother? According to Julia Kristeva, woman needs language, the paternal, symbolic order, to protect herself from the lack of distinction from the mother. As long as Irigaray speaks, given the rules of grammar, given the symbolic order of language, a first and a second person can be distinguished. The breakdown of these differences is mortally threatening. Kristeva writes in *Des Chinoises*, 'a woman has nothing to laugh about when the symbolic order collapses. She can enjoy it if, identifying with the mother, vaginated body, she imagines herself thus to be the sublime repressed which returns in the fissures of the order. She can also easily die of it. . .if, without successful maternal identification, the symbolic paternal order were her only tie to life.'[2] Irigaray might not be paralyzed, might be able to laugh, if she could really allow herself to be reabsorbed into the mother, quit resisting the identification, allow the distinction between speaker and interlocutor to break down. But that would mean running the risk of death–loss of self, loss of identity, beyond that–loss of the comforting belief in the omnipotent Mother who guards and can ensure the daughter's life.

Unlike Irigaray, Kristeva can speak from the mother's position.

For example, she writes: 'What relation between me, or even more modestly my body and this internal fold-graft which, once the umbilical cord cut, is an inaccessible other? My body and... it. No relation.'[3] The first person pronoun belongs to the mother here. And the mother's dilemma is represented–the experience of an internal heterogeneity which she cannot command. Besides such specific examples of speaking from the mother's place, Kristeva's assertive style and her mastery of several difficult jargons give the appearance of 'knowledge' and authority. Kristeva presumes to the right to assert, to speak as if she 'knows'; Irigaray, writing in a tentative, interrogative tone, always speaks her minority, her inadequate command. Thus, in a first moment, it would seem exceedingly agreeable to set up a dialogue between Irigaray and Kristeva as a dialogue between daughter and mother.

But the impulse to make this a mother/daughter dialogue may be so agreeable precisely because it is a way of domesticating an even more complicated relation between two women. According to Kristeva, the relation to the mother is always, in some way, reproduced between women.[4] That is the ghost which parenthetically spoils Irigaray's idyll. To say 'Mother, I prefer a woman to you' is naively to believe one could ever totally separate the woman from the mother, could define femininity with no reference to maternity. It is naively to believe that one could ever totally separate the daughter from the mother, secure their separate identities. It is to deny that one's mother is a woman, to deny any identification with one's mother. Certainly it is a stultifying reduction to subsume femininity into the category of maternity. But it is an opposite and perhaps even equally defensive reduction to believe in some simple separation of the two categories. The relation to the other woman only approaches its full complexity with some recognition that the 'other woman' as well as oneself is and is not 'Mother'.

My wish to fix Irigaray and Kristeva into daughter and mother roles resembles Irigaray's need to keep the two distinct. It is unfortunately never so clear who is mother and who is daughter. Irigaray does see that: 'You look at yourself in the mirror. And your mother is already there. And soon your daughter [as] mother. Between the two what are you?...Just a scansion: the time when one becomes the other.... Only this liquid which leaves one and arrives in the other, and which has no name' (*Et l'une...*, pp. 14–15). But her text resists this loss of name by never blurring the pronouns. 'You' becomes the name of the mother, her fixed identity.

To assign Kristeva the mother's place is to ignore much of what she has said out of some desire to make things simple and secure, some desire to locate the mother and have her there. Although she has spoken from the mother's place, Kristeva has also denounced that place as vacant: 'The cells fuse, split, proliferate... in a body there is grafted, unmasterable, an other. And no one is there, in that space both double and foreign, to signify it.'[5] No one is there. The 'mother' is not master of this mysterious process; she no more understands and commands it than does the child. No one has the right, the authority, to signify the experience, to intend its meaning or represent it.

Kristeva posits the fraudulence of speaking from that place, and speaks from it none the less, assuming and exposing the inevitable fraudulence. Irigaray's refusal to speak from that place, her resentment of the power of that place, leaves the mother phallic, that is, leaves the mother her supposed omniscience and omnipotence. Kristeva's presumption to speak from the place which no one has the right to speak from, combined with her constant, lucid analysis of that place and the necessity of such a presumption, works to dephallicize the Mother.

Of course, it is more usual and more comfortable to associate the phallic with the Father. A feminist protest might be lodged that to speak of a 'phallic mother' is to subsume female experience into male categories. Kristeva, however, hangs on to the phallic categories. Perhaps it is this insistence on the seemingly paradoxical term 'phallic mother' which can most work to undo the supposedly natural logic of the ideological solidarity between phallus, father, power and man. The Phallic Mother is undeniably a fraud, yet one to which we are infantilely susceptible. If the phallus were understood as the veiled attribute of the Mother, then perhaps this logical scandal could expose the joint imposture of both Phallus and Mother.

The phallic mother is already present in the work of Freud and Lacan, but Kristeva emphasizes her. In *Polylogue* she writes: 'that every subject poses him/herself in relation to the phallus has been understood. But that the phallus is the mother: it is said, but here we are all *arrêtés* [stopped, arrested, fixed, stuck, paralyzed] by this "truth"' (p. 204). Is not this 'paralysis' akin to that of *Et l'une ne bouge pas...*? The idyllic space of women together is supposed to exclude the phallus. The assumption that the 'phallus' is male expects that the exclusion of males be sufficient to make a non-phallic space. The threat represented by the mother to this feminine idyll might be understood through the notion that Mother, though female, is none the less phallic. So, as an afterthought, not only men, but Mother must be expelled from the innocent, non-phallic paradise. The inability to separate the daughter, the woman, from the mother then becomes the structural impossibility of evading the Phallus.

According to Kristeva, the Primitive Father is 'more obvious than the phallic mother and, in that sense, less dangerous' (*Polylogue*, p. 212). Irigaray, who is so clever and agile in undermining various theoretical fathers, who has been, in the present book, the model for a daughter's strategies against patriarchy, is paralyzed by Mother. The phallic mother is more dangerous because less obviously phallic. If the phallus 'can only play its role when veiled' (Lacan),[6] then the phallic mother is more phallic precisely by being less obvious.

Perhaps Kristeva's most powerful subversion is to expose the phallus of the phallic mother. Not merely to theorize the phallic mother, but to theatricalize her, give her as spectacle, open the curtain. In earlier chapters, I have said that the most radical effect of Lacan is his assumption of the phallic position, his speaking as 'subject presumed to know', his acting like a prick, which in its audacity (for example, his 1980 unilateral dissolution of the Freudian School of Paris) exposes the necessary imposture of any occupant of the phallic, paternal, authority position. Is not Kristeva as she speaks from the necessarily vacant position of the Mother like Lacan who has the presumption to say 'Me, Truth, I speak'?[7]

Kristeva's presumption often takes the form of her text's drawing attention to her self, her body, her individual history in the midst of some larger theoretical discussion. According to the classic psychoanalytic view, female sexuality is narcissistic. A good description of such a female narcissistic economy can be found in Béla Grunberger's 'Outline for a Study of Narcissism in Female Sexuality' in *Female Sexuality: New Psychoanalytic Views*. Female sexuality can be characterized by continual reference to the self and the body, a continual drawing attention back to the body/self, an economy that Grunberger calls concentric. The surprising self-references that interrupt Kristeva's efforts to erect a theory might be seen as the marks of a female sexual economy, just as Lacan's sadistic cockiness can be seen as versions of a traditional male sexual economy.

An example of Kristeva's self-pleasuring reference to her body can be found at the beginning of *Des Chinoises*, a book precisely about the dangers of using oneself as a measure for the other. She mentions that she 'attributed her cheekbones to some Asiatic ancestor' (p. 14). Later in that book she refers to herself as 'neither Asiatic nor European, not recognized by the Chinese women and detached from the European men' (pp. 177–8). She thus has the cheek to constitute herself in the privileged position by which she alone might be able to bridge the abyss of otherness, to contact and report the heterogeneous. Is this not similar to her characterization of the uncanny experience of mothering?–'No one is there, in that space both double and foreign, to signify it' (*Polylogue*, p. 409). Is not her position as neither man nor woman, neither Asiatic nor European, in a similar 'space both double and foreign'?

In a article called 'A New Kind of Intellectual: The Dissident' (*Tel Quel*, 77), she posits a continual, analytic vigilant dissidence to any order as the necessary position for the intellectual. In this context she speaks of exile as dissidence and goes on to consider exile a necessary condition to attain to the irreligious state from which one would always be in opposition to any homogenation. The exile, by being in the place where she is out-of-place, always represents a heterogeneous exception to the constitution of a homogeneous group. And of course, she reminds us 'I speak a language of exile'. Kristeva is a Bulgarian living, working and writing in France and in French. So once again she is in the privileged position of marginality, in the position to represent heterogeneity, 'in that space both double and foreign, to signify it'.

(But how vulgar to flaunt it.)

As I read 'A New Kind of Intellectual', I grope to assert my right to be a 'dissident' without leaving my homeland and my native language, trying to arrange an interpretation of my position as one of exile too. Me too. Just like Mummy. My feminism and my psychoanalysis are French although I am American. My exile is even more profound because I speak a foreign language in my native language. America itself is become a foreign country for me. I cannot be so easily assigned to the category of foreigner, the allotted space for the heterogeneous which complements the homogeneous group. And so on.

As I anxiously seek my own claim to 'dissidence', to being 'a new kind of intellectual', to 'exile', am I not in some sort of trans-ference onto Kristeva, some archaic transference onto the phallic mother, 'more dangerous than the Primitive Father', seeking some reason for my own existence beyond the woman who is everything?...And I find plenty of reasons, lots of space. She is Bulgarian; I am American. I do not have Asiatic cheekbones. It is much easier to distinguish myself from Kristeva than from Iriga-ray who speaks as 'woman' without any specifications.

Just as Lacan's sadistic capriciousness reveals the prick behind the Phallus, the male sexuality behind the supposedly neutral position of authority; so Kristeva's narcissistic self-reference reveals the specific woman (the vulgar Bulgar), the female self-pleasuring body, behind the Mother. The phallic position, ac-cording to Kristeva, cannot be avoided. The most subtle, diffuse play will always erect itself. But if 'the phallus can play its role only when veiled', then to refuse and deny the phallic position may mean to veil it and be all the more phallic, whereas blatant-ly, audaciously, vulgarly to assume it may mean to dephallicize.

At the end of *Des Chinoises*, Kristeva speaks of such a knowing-ly fraudulent assumption of the position of power: 'a *power* assumed (and not *represented*) by a woman, is already a power that has a body...*unrepresentable* power' (pp. 226–7). A body as body cannot represent power. In its diversity and contradiction, it is always inadequate to the monolithic solidity of power. To assume power as a body is to exercise it without veiling (phalli-cizing) the inadequation between the body and the solid homo-geneity of power. Since, in the dialectic we live, a woman is more 'body', more contradictory, soft and polymorphous, whereas the diversity of a male body is more repressed so as to become phallic, powerful, tough and hard, firm and steady, for a woman as woman to assume power is to introduce a crack in the representa-tion of power.

'A power thus that no one represents, and not woman either. But which is recognized by and for each, assumed by and for each: man and woman; men and women only exercising it in order to criticize it...to make it move [*bouger*] (ibid., p. 228). It is no answer, no sure-fire solution to have women rather than men assume the position of power. Women are *not* so essentially and immutably 'body' that they are eternally and dependably unrepresentable. In a certain dialectical moment, a certain here and now, the assumption of power by women may crack the impassive, neuter mask of power. But were women to assume power, the representation of power would inevitably alter so as to reassimilate the contradiction, to suture the chink. Perhaps the conflict is always between body—as the inadequate name of some uncommanded diversity of drives and contradictions—and Power, between body and Law, between body and Phallus, even between body and Body. The second term in each pair is a finished, fixed representation. The first that which falls short of that representation.

Kristeva uses the same verb (*bouger*) as Irigaray's title. *Et l'une ne bouge pas sans l'autre* begins: 'With your milk, Mother, I have drunk *la glace*.' 'La glace' can mean both 'ice' and 'mirror'. The fluid from the mother which is necessary for life contains both ice, that which fixes and paralyzes movement, and a mirror, a representation. In Lacan's mirror-stage the infant is fixed, constrained in a representation which the infant believes to be the Other's, the mother's, image of her. The representation freezes the nameless flow ('Only this liquid which leaves one and arrives in the other, and which has no name'—Irigaray, p. 15). Yet without representation there is only infantile passivity, powerlessness, anxiety.[8] The only way to move is to exercise power *and* criticize it, not let it gel into a rigid representation.

Each must exercise *and* criticize the power; each must be both mother and daughter, both Father and woman ('Father' is the usual name for the veil which makes mother phallic, for that which covers and oppresses the mother, but which is also her phallus precisely by covering her). To avoid the paralysis of an infantile, oceanic passivity one must exercise. But to avoid the opposite paralysis of a rigid identity one must criticize. And the process cannot, must not stop. There must be a 'permanent alternation: never one without the other' (*Des Chinoises*, p. 44). Kristeva too is saying 'l'une ne bouge pas sans l'autre', one cannot move without the other. What for Irigaray is a desperate inextricability is, for Kristeva, affirmed and even celebrated as the condition for movement: 'never one without the other'.

'An impossible dialectic of two terms, a permanent alternation: never one without the other. It is not certain that someone is

capable of it here, now. An analyst attentive to history, to politics? A politician plugged into the unconscious? Perhaps, a woman
. . .' (ibid.). A psychoanalyst can criticize power; a politician
exercise it. Yet in order to move we must never have one without
the other.[9] The mutual incompatibility of psychoanalysis and
politics leads to paralyzing representations. Power rigidly resists
all criticism and becomes totalitarian. Psychoanalysis supposedly
flees the exercise of power only to create psychoanalytic institutions which codify correct representations of the unconscious and
becomes arenas for violent power struggles as well as forces of
oppression over analysands and analysts who do not conform.
'Never one without the other', knowingly, lucidly to exercise and
and criticize power is to dephallicize, to assume the phallus and
unveil that assumption as presumption, as fraud. A constantly
double discourse is necessary, one that asserts and then questions.
Who is capable of such duplicity? 'Perhaps a woman. . .'

So Kristeva dares to dream. A dangerous dream, one that will
later be contradicted–'A power thus that no one represents *and
not women either*' (p. 228). But on page 44, Kristeva dreams
toward the erection of woman as the unique being (the phallic is
always the realm of unicity) capable of the 'impossible dialectic of
two terms'. Woman is double; she is the 'space both double and
foreign' of maternity. The ellipsis following 'Perhaps a woman' is
the veil that erects the phallic mother, a woman who could command the dialectic of self and self-loss, of identity and heterogeneity. In the very moment that Kristeva posits 'never one without the other' she is led past the contradictory figures – analyst–
politician or politician–analyst – to the dream of a single, unified,
self-sufficient woman. What better illustration of the inevitability
of phallic erection in even the most lucid dephallicization.

At the end of a text called 'L'Autre du sexe',[10] Kristeva de-
nounces what seems just such a dream. She has posited that one
can be a mother *and* an artist and deplores the societal distribution of separate roles, mother or artist. But she then goes on to a
cautionary note as she envisions the suturing representation by
which society has already begun to accept these mother–artists.
'How true it is also that all these powers lean, in the end, on those
modern totalities that are mothers who "create" and who become
"responsible", bosses, officials. But, I think that, on the other
hand, the maternal function can be the apprenticeship of modesty and of a permanent calling into question; and if a woman lives

maternity and her artist's work thus, far from being a totalizing Mother–Goddess, she is rather a locus of vulnerability, of calling into question of oneself and of languages' (p. 40).

The Mother–Goddess, totalizing and phallic, must not be the goal–which is to say, the co-optation–of women's liberation. The experience of motherhood is not the phallic experience that the child supposes it to be. Rather it is an experience of vulnerability–'in a body there is grafted, unmasterable, an other' (*Polylogue*, p. 409). 'In a body' that the woman is accustomed to think of as her own, there is an other which cannot be hers. The mother calls herself as totality, as self, into question because within 'her' is something she does not encompass, that goes beyond her, is other. This experience, Kristeva thinks, might prepare her for a general, 'permanent calling into question'.

Yet has she not in her very alternative to the phallic mother, 'totalizing Mother-Goddess', simply posited another perfect creature, the mother as permanent 'dissident', as she who is able to give up her attachment to the symbolic order and constantly be on the side of criticism? Maternity is still in a privileged position. The supposed 'apprenticeship of modesty' gives rise to a rather immodest claim.

Has Kristeva forgotten that a mother is also a daughter, a woman who thus 'has nothing to laugh about when the symbolic order collapses' (*Des Chinoises*, p. 35)? Is she suggesting a self-martyring, self-sacrificing position, that the woman be constantly opposed to that which she needs for comfort and identity? Hardly likely to oppose the order, woman indeed clings to the symbolic so as not to be reabsorbed by the mother. Of course Kristeva presents an alternative: 'She can enjoy [the collapse] if, identifying with the mother...she imagines herself thus to be the sublime repressed which returns in the fissures of the order' (ibid.). This would seem to be Kristeva's strategy in the passage from 'L'Autre du sexe'; she is imagining the mother–artist to be the 'sublime repressed'. That may be a way to 'enjoy' the collapse of the symbolic order, but it is an imagining, the erection of a fantasy. The mother, even the mother–artist, is no more safely ensconced on the side of contestation than is anyone. Any position can become assimilated into the symbolic order as a codified, fixed representation. No 'experience' or 'identity' can guarantee one's dissidence. As Kristeva herself so clearly puts it: 'once represented, be it under the aspect of a woman, the "truth" of the unconscious

passes into the symbolic order. . . . The vulgar but oh how effective trap of "feminism": to recognize ourselves, to make of us The
Truth . . . so as to keep us from functioning as [the order's]
unconscious "truth"' (ibid., p. 42). Kristeva too can fall into this
'trap of feminism'. In fact it is the constant companion that
threatens her theoretical work.

One of the most important notions in Kristevan theory is that
of 'the semiotic'. Starting from Lacan's notion of 'the symbolic' as
the order of language, the paternal order which locates each
subject, Kristeva goes on to posit a more archaic dimension of
language, pre-discursive, pre-verbal, which has to do with
rhythm, tone, colour, with all that which does not simply serve
for representation. The semiotic is a more immediate expression
of the drives and is linked to the bodily contact with the mother
before the paternal order of language comes to separate subject
from mother. Although it can be examined clearly in the sounds
produced by pre-linguistic infants, the semiotic is always tra-
versing language, always a bodily presence disruptive to the sublimated symbolic order. The semiotic is given freer play in works
of 'art': it is the poetic dimension of language. But just because
the semiotic always harks back to the pre-Oedipal relation to the
mother, that does not mean that a mother as speaking subject in
the symbolic order is somehow on the side of the semiotic, that
does not make her a representative of the semiotic. The semiotic
is the locus of force, revolution and art in Kristeva's work, clearly
'where the action is', and she runs the risk of believing the mother
in command of the semiotic.

In thinking about Kristevan theory, there arises the question of
the relation between 'the semiotic' and the Lacanian 'imaginary'.
Both are defined in contradistinction to 'the symbolic'. Both are
associated with the pre-Oedipal, pre-linguistic maternal. But
whereas the imaginary is conservative and comforting, tends toward closure, and is disrupted by the symbolic; the semiotic is
revolutionary, breaks closure, and disrupts the symbolic. It
seems there are two kinds of maternals; one more conservative
than the paternal symbolic, one less. It is noteworthy that the
male theorist sees the paternal as disruptive, the maternal as
stagnant, whereas the female theorist reverses the positions.

The danger in Kristeva's theory is that 'the semiotic' fall into
'the imaginary'—in other words, that the potential disruption of
the maternal becomes the alibi for what actually functions as a

comforting representation. The incompatibility of Lacanian and Kristevan theories, the difficulty in thinking a relation between the 'imaginary' and the 'semiotic', ought to be attended to as a locus of conflict between two maternals—one conservative, the other dissident—as a way of keeping the position of the mother 'both double and foreign', of guarding against a complacent assimilation of the mother to one side or the other, against a smug attribution of superior dissidence to one sex over the other.

To think the contradictory relation between Kristevan and Lacanian theory might mean a possibility of thinking the impossible relation between the sexes, of heterosexual rather than homological thinking. Any discourse phallicizes, but somehow it is in the possibility of a dialogue between two heterogeneous discourses that the 'impossible dialectic of two terms' might be found. No one (as one) can speak the double discourse of the 'permanent alternation: never one without the other'. No one person can think heterosexually, but it may be that Kristeva provides an example of a heterosexual text in the article 'Polylogue' found in the book by the same title. There, the woman theorist's words lie with those of a male artist. Kristeva's discourse is interpenetrated by the words of her husband Philippe Sollers. And something quite exciting occurs.

'Polylogue' is Kristeva's reading of Sollers's novel *H.* The 'something quite exciting' happens neither in the beginning where we read Kristeva's theoretical discourse about Sollers nor at the end when we are given three pages of *H* to read, uninterrupted by Kristeva. The zone of excitement is in the middle of 'Polylogue' where it becomes impossible to find any complete statement that does not include words from both Kristeva and Sollers. In this zone, the two discourses cannot be separated and still make sense ('never one without the other'), and yet their doubleness remains marked by the quotations around Sollers's words. In this midsection, specifically in a passage spanning pages 210 and 211, there is beautiful, exciting talk of a 'new love', a heterosexual marriage that would not be a fusion of two into one. And the passage on that marriage *is* that marriage.

In my enthusiasm, I am much tempted to quote that passage, although over a page long, in its entirety. I have trouble thinking of representing it in my own words (fear of inadequate representation, fraudulence?). Yet my dilemma about quotation participates in the very dialectic at stake here. To represent another text is to assimilate the other's discourse into one's own, to re-establish a single economy. But in an opposite and perhaps equally defensive homogenization, to efface one's own discourse and simply quote *in extenso* leaves us once again with a single economy. The 'new love', a heterosexuality that is not 'mythic fusion' (Kristeva, loc. cit.), might be a text that alternately quotes and comments, exercises and criticizes. The defences against 'love', including love for a text, are either to find the beloved so beautiful that s/he be left untouched, veiled, phallic (uninterrupted quotation) or to want to possess totally, to appropriate the desirable other so as to silence one's troubling desire, to master the otherness that has gotten under one's skin. Kristeva's intercourse with *H* begins with one defence (representation) and ends with the other (pure quotation), but in between there is a hot encounter.

In this passage Sollers says 'I want to see people *jouir* while seeking why.' 'Jouir' is often associated with the maternal, the body, the semiotic, that which is outside the symbolic order. 'Seeking why' gives theory, philosophy, is the site of the most sublimated, most symbolic, least semiotic language. The 'new love' must be *jouissance* and theory. *Jouissance* (pleasure, enjoyment) without analysis leads to mystification, 'mythic fusion', God, the One, the Phallus. But to enjoy *while* seeking why is vigilantly to keep the double discourse, to resist mystification, religion, phallicization.

Kristeva is a theoretician: her words a continual 'seeking why'. Sollers is a 'poet', which, according to Kristeva means one who embraces the semiotic, choosing to enter the rhythmic maternal, whose language is closer to *jouissance*. In a first moment, it would seem exceedingly agreeable to align Kristeva/theory with 'seeking why' and Sollers/poetry with 'jouir'. But the semiotic traverses even the most sublimated theory, and Sollers' writing is not just play but a continual thinking. Heterosexuality is not simply the meeting of two opposites which keep their opposite identities, but an intermingling of two opposites, a contamination of the opposition, a risking of difference and identity, that risk not being offset by some higher union, the oneness of the homogeneous 'couple'.

It is noteworthy that in this marriage the paternal, symbolic, theoretical discourse is written by the woman, whereas the maternal, semiotic, poetic discourse issues from the man's pen. A woman theoretician is already an exile; expatriated from her *langue maternelle*, she speaks a paternal language; she presumes to a fraudulent power. A male poet such as Sollers, by choosing to explore the rhythmic, writes as a representative of the maternal: his position is likewise fraud. Each is already double, already duplicitous; but no identity, no role reversal, no exile can guarantee a position of permanent, irrecoverable dissidence. Yet perhaps the doubling of their duplicity, the encounter of a female and a male modality of dissidence, the intercourse of a male and a female bisexuality, has a greater chance of carrying on the 'impossible dialectic of two terms'.

(At this point of reflection upon the doubly duplicitous discourse, in my meditation on this example of heterotextuality, I am stuck, stymied, paralyzed. There are two paths of inquiry that beckon. But I cannot choose one. The right path to take leads to the mother and something that worries me. But in planning to proceed down the right path, there remains a desire or a need or a compulsion for the path which is left. The one left leads to the lesbian and something that worries Kristeva. The only way I can move from this spot is to do both–'never one without the other'.)

A militant, feminist question nags me. How can you privilege a relation called 'heterosexuality?' Does this not support the heterosexism of our culture, the oppression of homosexuals, the repression of homosexuality? Of course, I wish to speak of a radical heterosexuality, a true openness and love for the *heteros*, the other, an intercourse between two modalities. As we saw with Irigaray what has been called heterosexuality has always been a veiled homosexuality, one modality of desire, one libidinal economy. And any relation between members of the same sex which allowed their difference, did not assimilate both to one fantasy, would be heterosexual. But we cannot be sure that this radical notion of 'heterosexuality' is not just an alibi for the

Kristeva has published another double discourse. Once again in 'L'Héréthique de l'amour' we find rhythmic, poetic language lying side by side with theoretical, discursive prose. But this time Kristeva authors both discourses. The continuous, discursive language is a scholarly investigation of the representation of the maternal in the Christian tradition. Alongside we find a discontinuous speaking of motherhood: sometimes speaking from the position of Mother (as commented upon above), sometimes from another position. Here then are two discourses: one double and one single, unified. The combination could be said to represent the maternal position. The speaking subject who is a mother is a being split between the singleness of the comforting norm.

Kristeva certainly seems, at moments, to consider homosexuality a defence, a short-circuiting of the relation to heterogeneity, 'a safety-belt' ('L'autre du sexe', p. 37), a rigid, fragile phallic stand on identity, a fearful refusal of the mother, the vagina, and the semiotic.

In speaking of the Chinese erotic tradition, she distinguishes between two homosexualities: one that is acceptable to the Chinese tradition of a double sexual economy and one that is not. 'Feminine homosexuality like feminine masturbation are not "tolerated", they are unquestionable, they are "natural" ...what seems to cause problems, is the woman who cheats: she who passes for a man, who eliminates the *yin–yang* doublet in order to simply present herself as a male seducer more or less brutal and dominating' (*Des Chinoises*, p. 68). In the political terms earlier discussed, this bad homosexual woman would try to 'represent' power rather than merely 'assume' it. This same phallic woman who 'causes problems' for a traditional Chinese sexuality seems also to disturb Kristeva, to upset the author who desired 'to be recognized' by the Chinese women 'as one of them' (p. 177).

Indeed, this phallic woman already seems to be 'causing problems' in the beginning section of *Des Chinoises*, which is concerned with women here in the West. Kristeva is explaining the speaking subject (the totalizing 'I') and the doubleness experienced in maternity. Both single and double, the mother is already by herself a site of double doubling. The phrase Kristeva uses to speak of the maternal body, 'a space both double and foreign', bears witness to that double doubleness by the necessity for the two words 'both' and 'double'. Speaking from the maternal position can only be, as said earlier, a fraud, a duplicity. But speaking theory, the paternal symbolic is also fraud, especially for a woman who is thus alienated, exiled in a foreign language. Here again we have a double duplicity, two modalities of fraudulence, one paternal, one maternal.

But this time the woman–mother and theorist, in other words, 'both double and foreign' –can do it all alone. No Sollers, no male poet, no other person is necessary. She wrote in *Des Chinoises*, 'it is not certain that someone is capable [of the permanent alternation]...Perhaps, a woman...' (p. 44). The author of 'L'Héréthique' would seem to be that woman.

Yet this triumph is troubling. It is simply too reminiscent of a 'vulgar but oh how effective trap' of motherhood. Upon becoming a mother the woman, like a Queen Bee, loses all interest in her husband, in heterosexuality, and derives her gratification from her maternity. I fear that both the mother–child relation and the experience of one's own necessity for a woman to adopt a male stance in order to be heard, to have power: 'From Louise Michel to A. Kollontaï, to take only two relatively recent examples, not to mention the suffragettes or their current Anglo-Saxon sisters some of whom are more menacing than a father of the primitive horde—we can serve or overthrow the sociohistorical order by playing supermen. Some women delight in it: the most active, the most effective, the "homosexuals" (whether they know it or not)' (ibid., pp. 42-3).

The 'suffragettes' are included in a kind of compulsive digression by which she mentions what she will not mention. A further digression is added to the already gratuitous mention. The digression within the digression has an insistent force that perverts and deforms the sentence. The marginal detail, 'more menacing than a father of the primitive horde', sensationally detracts attention away from the main point of the sentence. That which she chooses 'not to mention' takes over the sentence as if she could not control anything so 'menacing'. The invasion of these mammoth, scary 'Anglo-Saxons' is so complete that at the conclusion of the sentence we find an English word. 'Supermen' appears, not even italicized, in Kristeva's French text.

Kristeva's only defence against this menacing, primitive invasion is the parenthesis in the next sentence: 'homosexuals (whether

otherness can be more easily contained in the imaginary, in a homogenized fantasy, a stagnant representation, than can a relation to another adult.

Kristeva seems to think not. 'That there is no sexual relation is a paltry finding before this flash that dazzles me faced with the abyss between what was mine and is henceforth only irremediably foreign' ('L'Héréthique', p. 44). 'That there is no sexual relation' is Lacan's great scandalous finding, his announcement of the impossibility of heterosexuality. Not disagreeing, Kristeva however thinks that a minor scandal, 'paltry' compared to the discovery of the abyss separating mother and child, separating the mother from what was herself.

Is Kristeva's move from the impossible heterosexuality of 'Polylogue' to the impossible maternity of 'L'Héréthique', in other words, is the move from the Lacanian scandal to the maternal scandal progress or regression? This question rejoins the problem of whether the maternal is conservative and imaginary or disruptive and semiotic. And uncomfortable as it is (precisely because it is uncomfortable) we must try to sit on the horns of that dilemma.

Of course, heterosexuality is always implied by maternity. Except in the case of the Virgin Mary, which is precisely the case Kristeva is investigating in 'L'Héréthique'. I fear Kristeva is acting out the Virgin Mother

they know it or not)'. These
Anglo-Saxons may be bigger and
scarier, but like some 'father of
the primitive horde' they are big
and dumb and do not 'know'
what the sophisticated Parisian
knows. As she faces the East,
brave in the encounter with the
Oriental other, a threat sneaks
up from behind, from the West.
Have we found, here, the phallic
mother with whom Kristeva cannot identify and who thus paralyzes her in rigid defence?

while writing about her and so I
search for some trace of male
penetration, perhaps out of my
own fears of precisely such a self-
sufficient mother. I am relieved
to find a trace of the previous
heterosexual encounter. Kristeva
has made up a word, 'Héréthique', to name her maternal textual production. The word is
rich in connotations: a conden-
sation of 'hérétique' (heretic)
and 'éthique' (ethics). But although altered in spelling, in
speech the made-up word in no

way differs from 'hérétique'. What has been added is a silent 'H', the
name of Sollers's text in 'Polylogue'.

Written language is a further mediation over oral, and it is in the
written, mediated, more symbolic dimension that we find the mark of
the father. That unpronounceable paternal, heterosexual presence
opens up the 'heretic' to 'ethics'. According to 'L'Héréthique', access
to ethics is 'access to the other' (p. 47).

Our encounter with Kristeva has returned again and again to a
similar suspicion, a mistrust of the Mother, of the occupant of the
Mother's place. Although at the very beginning, I posited the
effective, revolutionary strategy of Kristeva's audacious assumption of that place, the suspicions return. Just as in my reading of
Lemoine-Luccioni's *Partage des femmes* it became clear that a
woman is never quite sure that a penis is not a Phallus, can never
stably separate the male from the phallic; so it becomes obvious
that one has a similar problem believing the mother is not phallic,
trusting other women not to reabsorb, not especially to be in command of the reabsorption which threatens each one.

It is not enough, although I think it is a lot, to speak the scandal, speak from the scandalous place of the Phallic Mother as self-
pleasuring body (as Kristeva does) or the place of Phallic Authority as capricious prick (as Lacan does). Despite their blatant fraudulence, they will always find believers (among which, above all,
the resenters, those most obstinate of believers). The need, the
desire, the wish for the Phallus is great. No matter how oppressive

its reign, it is much more comforting than no one in command.

9　Keys to Dora

In 1976 a book was published in France, on the cover of which we read: 'Portrait de Dora/de Hélène Cixous/des femmes'. These three lines are repeated on the title page, but there 'des femmes' is followed by an address—2 rue de la Roquette 75011 Paris, for it is the name of a publishing house, linked with the woman's group called 'Psychoanalysis and Politics'. As the name of a press, 'des femmes' appears on many books, but it seems particularly resonant on this cover where it occasions the third occurrence of the preposition 'de' (of, from). The unusual inclusion of a 'de' before the author's name works to draw the heroine Dora, the author, Hélène Cixous, as well as the press's name, that is 'women', into a circuit of substitution embodied in the grammatical structure of apposition. The portrait of Dora is also a portrait of Hélène Cixous is also a portrait of women (in general).

According to the dictionary, a 'portrait' is a 'representation of a real person'. 'Representation' has a theatrical as well as a visual sense, and Cixous's text is a play, a theatrical script. But 'portrait' also has an interesting figurative sense. The dictionary (*Le Petit Robert*) gives the following example from Balzac: 'Virginie était tout le *portrait de* sa mère' (emphasis mine), as we say in English, 'Virginia was the (spitting) image of her mother.' 'Portrait' itself leads us not only to representation in the visual and theatrical senses, but to re-presentation, replication, the substitutability of one woman for another.

Dora is Freud's Dora, the name Freud gives to the heroine of his 'Fragment of an Analysis of a Case of Hysteria', published in 1905. In this case-history, Freud writes of Dora's complaint that she is being used as an 'object of barter'. Dora protests that her father has handed her over to his friend in exchange for that friend's wife. Freud does not disagree with Dora's inference, but merely states that this is not a 'formal agreement' between the two men, but one that the men do without being conscious of it. Dora and Freud have discovered a fragment of the general structure

132

which thirty years later Claude Lévi-Strauss will call elementary
kinship structures, that is the exchange of women between men.
Lévi-Strauss's formulation of this general system of exchange is
structuralism's major contribution to feminist theory.

In another book, *La jeune née*, which has become a major text
of French feminist theory, Cixous writes, 'I am what Dora would
have been if the history of women [*histoire des femmes*] had
begun.'[1] The *histoire* (history, story) that intervenes is *des
femmes*, taking that phrase as both objective and subjective geni-
tive. The cover of *Portrait* imposes a double reading of the 'de' in
'des femmes', since it follows two opposing uses of the preposition.
The history of women must also be a history by women, women
making their own history. *Histoire des femmes*: a story coming
from women, a story published by the press *des femmes* (what
Anglophone feminists call 'herstory') alters the identification
between Dora and Cixous. By passing through the terms 'des
femmes', whose generality appropriately designates a press, that
which places words in general circulation, the triple identification
saves Cixous from being simply another Dora, as Dora was rather
than as she 'would have been'.

La jeune née is comprised of three sections: the first by Catherine Clément, the second by Hélène Cixous, the third an unpre-
pared, unedited dialogue between the two. Throughout *La jeune
née* the hysteric, particularly Dora, functions as an insistent
question the two women writers are asking: Is she a heroine or a
victim?

At the beginning of the book, Clément declares that the role of
the hysteric is ambiguous: she both contests and conserves (p. 13).
The hysteric contests inasmuch as she 'undoes family ties, introduces perturbation into the orderly unfolding of daily life, stirs up
magic in apparent reason' (pp. 13–14). But the hysteric's contestation is contained and co-opted, and, like any victory of the
familiar, the familial over the heterogeneous and alien, this containment serves to strengthen the family. 'Every hysteric ends up
inuring the others to her symptoms, and the family closes up once
more around her' (p. 14). The family assimilates her otherness,
and like an amoeba, finds its single cell revitalized, stronger than
before.

Thus upon its first appearance the question of the hysteric's
role seems answered, resolved into an irresolvable but stable and
determinable ambiguity. Yet as the book continues, the ambi-

guity defined by Clément seems not so stable, not so easy to declare and accept as such. Just as the hysteric perturbs the orderly
unfolding of family life, might she not likewise disturb the position of authorial mastery in this book? This cannot be considered
a failing in a book where the desirability of a masterful authorial
discourse is itself called into question. But to be unseated by
hysteria is not the same as to give up intentionally one's masterful
position. The reasonable, forceful, clever position for the two women theorists is to assume the inevitability of ambiguity. To
choose ambiguity is to choose to give up one's masterful position,
is simply a ruse toward a more resilient mastery. Yet rather than
assume the ambiguity, the two writers themselves become pola-
rized as advocates of *either* the hysteric as contesting *or* the
hysteric as conserving.

During a discussion of the hysteric's role, Clément says to
Cixous, 'Listen, you really like Dora, but as for me, she has never
seemed to me to be a revolutionary heroine.' To which Cixous
replies, 'I don't give a damn about Dora, I don't fetichize her. She
is the name of a certain disturbing force which means that the
little circus no longer runs' (p. 289). Cixous's testy, defensive
reply–'I don't give a damn...I don't fetichize her'–picks up, with
perhaps hysterical hypersensitivity, the implicit and personal
accusation in Clément's 'Listen, you really like Dora, but as for
me...' Clément needs to make her position clear, to distinguish
herself from Cixous, to distinguish between 'you' and 'me', and,
more urgently, to distinguish herself from Cixous's identification
with Dora.

Whereas Cixous can write 'the hysterics are my sisters' (p. 184),
in the same book Clément declares, 'Physically [the hysterics] are
no longer...and if some one dresses up like one, it is a disguise.
They are obsolete figures...I really liked them, but they no
longer exist' (p. 111). Clément writes 'I really liked them' in the
past tense, whereas she later says to Cixous 'you really like Dora'
in the present tense. The disagreement seems to be a struggle to
keep the hysteric an 'obsolete figure', to keep the hysterical identification in the past.

To understand more fully this outburst–'I don't give a damn
...I don't fetichize her'–let us follow the argument in the pages
immediately preceding this moment:

Cixous asserts that 'it is very difficult to block this sort of person
who leaves you no peace, who makes permanent war against you'

(p. 287). War functions in Cixous's section of the book as a positive value, necessary for transformation. If the hysteric makes 'permanent war', leaves 'no peace', then she must be safely ensconced on the side of contestation, unambiguously non-assimilable. But to Cixous's assertion, Clément replies: 'Yes, that introduces dissension, but it in no way makes anything burst; that does not *disperse* the bourgeois family which only exists through her dissension: which only holds together in the possibility or the reality of its own disturbance, always re-closable, always re-closed' (ibid., Clément's italics). The contesting hysteric is thus necessary to the family cell and serves a conservative function. Rather than seeing the hysteric's role as ambiguous, Clément now argues that it is only deluded, co-opted rebellion. She may appear to disturb, but the hysteric actually provides an opportunity for the family to revitalize itself through the assimilation of something outside itself. She feeds the family machine. A heroine for Cixous, Clément considers Dora only a victim.

According to Clément (p. 288), the difference between those whose violence is re-assimilable and those whose contestation is effective lies in the attainment of 'symbolic inscription'. The Lacanian term 'symbolic' which Clément uses here is in contradistinction to the term 'imaginary'. Whereas the imaginary is a closed circle, the 'symbolic' opens out into a generalized exchange. Lacan takes the term 'symbolic' from Lévi-Strauss. Lévi-Strauss's kinship structures belong to the symbolic order whereas Dora's and Freud's fragment of those structures remain within the particular family as a perverse exception. Mirroring, one-to-one identification typifies the imaginary register. Following Clément's standard of 'symbolic inscription' we can see that Cixous''s identification with Dora is saved from the circular delusions and powerlessness of the imaginary because it passes through the third term on the cover, passes through the press *des femmes*. Once published, the scandal can no longer be contained within the family. Publication 'disperses', to use the word Clément emphasizes. The circle of the family is broken, the cell walls burst.

For Clément, Dora does not pass into 'symbolic inscription', and so Dora's outbursts burst nothing. According to Clément: 'Raising a ruckus, causing a crisis, perturbing familial relations, that is re-closable.' But Cixous responds, 'And it is that very force which works in the dismantling of structures.... Dora broke something.' Clément replies: 'I don't think so' (pp. 288–9).

The disagreement turns around the question of whether something is broken or not, open or closed. In a footnote to the Dora case, Freud writes: 'the question whether a woman is "open" or "shut" can naturally not be a matter of indifference'.[2] The question of open or shut cannot be left undecided, ambiguous. Clément has articulated the question of whether a woman contests or conserves around the distinction open or shut. Although Clément begins by defining the hysteric's position as ambiguous, once it is tied to the question 'open or shut' that ambiguity becomes intolerable; it must be decided. As in Freud's footnote, what is at stake is a woman's honour. Is Dora compromised or not?

Still and all, from Freud's footnote to *La jeune née*, things have changed. For Clément and Cixous, the heroine is she who has broken something. In the 1975 text, compromise attaches to the woman who is shut up; whereas in Freud's context it is the open woman whose honour is compromised. This is not a simple reversal of values: a shift in grammatical position alters the opposition in a manner more complex than reversal. In Freud's question the woman is, in either case, grammatically passive: she remains passively 'shut' or she is 'open' through an outside agent, a man. But in *La jeune née*, that which cannot be 'a matter of indifference' involves a difference in the woman's grammatical position. Does she 'open' the family, or is she 'shut' by it? The 1975 question 'open' or 'shut' includes a second question, the question of woman as agent or patient. In Freud's text she can only be patient, in fact, Doctor Freud's patient. But just as the agent of the 'Portrait' (de Hélène Cixous) can identify/be identified with the patient of the 'Portrait' (de Dora), the advent of the 'histoire des femmes', the case-history of and by women, gives the woman the agency to open, allows her to do more than patiently wait for a determination of what can 'naturally' not be a matter of indifference.

The distinction 'open' or 'shut' matters in the book *La jeune née*. Cixous's section is entitled 'Sorties', which can be translated as 'exits, outlets, escapes, holidays, outings, sallies, sorties', also 'outbursts, attacks and tirades'. Let us remark especially the warlike and the hysterical senses ('attack'), but in general there is a sense of exits, openings, escapes from enclosures. Also: the disagreement between Clément and Cixous is located in a published dialogue. The choice to publish a 'dissension', bring it to 'symbolic inscription', is the choice to leave it open, not try to re-assimilate it, shut it up, or keep it within the family.

Freud's open-and-shut footnote specifically refers to Dora's concern over whether a door is locked or not, which comes up in her associations to the 'first dream' of the case. Freud's footnote extends the door metaphor: 'The question whether a woman is "open" or "shut" can naturally not be a matter of indifference. It is well known, too, what sort of "key" effects the opening in such a case.' Cixous has Freud speak these two sentences to Dora in the play. Dora says, 'when I wanted... to close myself in to rest no more key! I am sure it was Mr. K who had taken it away.' Freud then pronounces the two sentences, to which Dora replies, 'I was "sure" you would say that!' (pp. 48–9). The two 'sure's'–the second one in quotation marks, apparently a quote from the first one–connect Dora's certainty about K's culpable intentions and her certainty about Freud, bringing out her substitution of Freud for K in the transference.

Later in his text on Dora, Freud writes, 'sexuality is the key to the problem of the psychoneuroses and of the neuroses in general. No one who disdains the key will ever be able to unlock the door' (p. 115). That the 'well-known', 'natural' sexual imagery of the footnote should recur in Freud's discussion of his own enterprise seems to bear out Dora's suspicion that Freud is somehow in the position of Herr K. Both hold the key and are threatening to unlock the door.

Portrait's framing of the footnote sentences with Dora's two 'sure's' also brings out the smug certitude of Freud's 'naturally' and his 'well-known'. Is this not the worst sort of vulgar, predict-able 'Freudian' interpretation? The predictability of Freud's line about keys offends Dora by denying the specificity of her signifiers (by not attending to her, but merely applying general formulas) in the same way that she is offended by Herr K's beginning his declaration of love with what she knew were the same words he had used to seduce a governess. What woman wants to be opened by a skeleton key?

Cixous says of the case of Dora, 'I immediately operated a reading that was probably not centred as Freud wanted it to be.... I read it as a fiction' (*La jeune née*, p. 272). Freud begins the case-history with instructions as to how it ought to be read. It ought to be read scientifically; but even as he writes it, he is aware there will be those readers who pervert (Cixous would say 'decentre') his intentions, who read it for pleasure. From Freud's Preface to the Dora case: 'I am aware that—in this city, at least—there are many physicians who (revolting though it may seem) choose to read a case history of this kind not as a contribution to the psychopathology of neuroses, but as a *roman à clef* designed for their private delectation' (p. 9). The English translation borrows a French expression to render Freud's 'Schlüsselroman', literally 'key-novel'. The vulgar, perverse reading Freud fears would entail looking for 'keys' in his text, as one would in a novel (Cixous's 'fiction').

Somehow the base, the vulgar in the Dora case is connected three times to 'keys'. (1) The vulgar, 'revolting' reading looks for keys (p. 9); (2) Freud's footnote refers to the 'well-known' symbolism of keys (p. 67), thus himself giving a common, vulgar interpretation; and (3) finally, we are told in the Postface that 'sexuality is the key' (p. 115). Freud knows that many will 'disdain' this key, that is, find it 'revolting', vulgar, below them. Is not his disgust at his vulgar readers, who read for their own 'delectation', a similar gesture of contempt for the sexual, particularly for the perverse—those components of sexuality which simply give pleasure as opposed to work for reproduction (cf. 'read not as a contribution but for their delectation')? Perhaps Cixous's decentring, perverse reading of Dora as a fiction of keys recovers the 'revolting', scandalous force of Freud's discovery of infantile, perverse sexuality.

It is interesting to note that the kind of reading Freud expected and dreaded from the physicians, 'of this city, at least', must be represented in the English translation by a French phrase, 'roman à clef'. In the eyes of the traditional English-speaking psychoanalytic community, the reading of Freud currently practised in France is likewise inappropriate and unscientific. The French are reading Freud literarily, as if it were a novel, paying attention to the letter of his text, to such trivial details as the repeated appearance of the word 'Schlüssel'. The inappropriateness of French Freud, however, seems to rejoin some original Viennese reading. The original German text did not need the French phrase. Perhaps, for those of us who read Freud in English, a French detour is necessary in order to recover the original, scandalous Viennese reading, in order not to lose the 'key'.

A French detour may be literally—that is, *à la lettre*—necessary.

The English translator chooses to use the French 'détour' rather than the English 'detour' for the German 'Umwege', that is, chooses to include the accute accent, in the following sentence from the Dora case: 'The dream, in short, is one of the *détours by which repression can be evaded*' (p. 15). Freud's German sentence has no italics; they originate in the English translation, as if this sentence were of particular importance to the English text, the English context. According to certain French psychoanalysts, particularly Lacan, English and American psychoanalysis has repressed the unconscious out of psychoanalysis. In that context the 'détour', the French detour, a detour through the French reading of Freud, *à la lettre*, is perhaps a means, a hope for evading repression, the repression of what is 'revolting', that is, original in Freud.

There is another equally apt occasion when the English translator finds it necessary to render Freud's German with a French phrase. Freud states that 'the determination of Dora's symptoms is far too specific for it to be possible to expect a frequent recurrence of the same accidental aetiology' (p. 40). This assertion puts into doubt the value of publishing this case-history, its value as 'a contribution'. 'Have we not merely allowed ourselves to become the victims of a *jeu d'esprit?*' asks Freud in the English translation. The French is occasioned by the German 'Spiel des Witzes'. Anglophone psychoanalysis has often dismissed the current Parisian equivalent as unserious word-play, mere punning. The German word 'Witz' can be construed as an allusion to *Jokes and their Relation to the Unconscious (Der Witz. . .)*, published by Freud in the same year as the Dora case. The French have paid great attention to this jokebook as one of the best illustrations that what Freud discovered is an unconscious structured like a language.

Freud is here discussing the problem of the 'skeleton key', of the interpretation which fits many similar cases. Freud's radical discovery was the specificity expressed in every symptom. Yet the fate of psychoanalysis in the English-speaking countries where it achieved such popularity was to become a set system of interpretation, a ready-made symbolism to be applied to many cases, giving it an obvious market value, quieting the very doubt Freud expresses here. Again, it may be necessary to pass through the French 'jeu d'esprit' in order to rediscover Freud's discovery—that symptoms are ways of speaking, and like all communications, only take meaning in a specific context.[3] Just as Cixous's Dora refuses the substitutability of all women, psychoanalysis (and feminism) must refuse the substitutability of all cases, the 'well-known sort of key' ('It is *well known* what sort of "key" effects the opening in such a *case*').

It is not just the English translator who puts the Dora text through French detours; Freud himself interjected French phrases at certain points in his German text. The most remarkable one, one that Cixous writes into her play (p. 36), is the sentence 'J'appelle un chat un chat' (literally, 'I call a cat a cat', compare the English 'call a spade a spade'). The context is once again the question of scandal, here specifically that the reader might be scandalized that a psychoanalyst should discuss sexual practices, especially perverse sexual practices (in this case, oral intercourse) with an inexperienced girl.

Freud writes, 'A gynaecologist, after all, under the same conditions, does not hesitate to *make them submit to uncovering every possible part of their body*. The *best way* of speaking about such things *is to be dry and direct*' (my italics). Freud concludes his argument thus: 'I call bodily organs and processes by their technical names, and I tell these to the patient if they—the names, I mean—happen to be unknown to her. *J'appelle un chat un chat*' (p. 48). At the very moment he defines non-prurient language as direct and non-euphemistic, he takes a French detour into a figurative expression. By his terms, this French sentence would seem to be titillating, coy, flirtatious. And to make matters more juicy (less 'dry'), 'chat' or 'chatte' can be used as vulgar (vulvar) slang for the female genitalia. So in this gynaecological context, where he founds his innocence upon the direct use of technical terms, he takes a French detour and calls a pussy a pussy.[4]

Freud's defensive interjection, 'the names, I mean', leads us back to a passage where he writes that he 'took the greatest pains with this patient not to introduce her to any fresh facts in the region of sexual knowledge. . . I did not call a thing by its name until her allusions to it had become so unambiguous that there seemed slight risk in translating them into direct speech' (p. 31). Freud restricts his activities to translation from allusive to 'direct speech'. But as we have seen 'direct speech' leads to 'j'appelle un chat un chat', that is, translation from German into French, from scientific into figurative language, from original expression into cliché. The innocent activity Freud calls 'translation' seems to relate to some kind of suspicious *détour* which allows repression to be evaded.

The passage continues: 'Her answer was always prompt and frank: she knew about it already. But the question of where her knowledge came from was a riddle which her memories were unable to solve' (ibid.). Freud is *not* the author of her knowledge (merely the translator), but who is? As translator of an anonymous text, his responsibility (or lack of it) is more ambiguous. The 'riddle' is not solved until it is too late, until a footnote to the Postface where Freud writes, 'I *ought to have* guessed that the main source of her knowledge of sexual matters could have been no one but Frau K...I *ought to have* attacked this riddle and looked for the motive of *such an extraordinary* piece of repression' (p. 120n, my italics). Why did Freud fail to do what he 'ought to have'? Why did he not attack the riddle?

In *Portrait de Dora*, Freud's line 'J'appelle un chat un chat' is spoken by Frau K (p. 36). This sets up an identification between the 'author' of Dora's sexual knowledge and its 'translator'. Is Freud afraid of solving the riddle because, like Oedipus, he will find himself to be the guilty party?

In a way, yes. But not because of any direct identification with Frau K. Before he finally solves the riddle, Freud arrives at a preliminary solution. 'For some time', Freud writes in a footnote, 'I looked upon [Dora's governess] as the source of all Dora's secret knowledge, and perhaps I was not entirely wrong in this' (p. 36n). It is precisely in the position of the governess, of the servant, that Dora places Freud.

When Dora announces that they are in their last session, Freud asks her when she decided to terminate the analysis. To her response, 'a fortnight ago', Freud replies, 'that sounds just like a maidservant or a governess—a fortnight's warning'. Is the servant giving two weeks' notice before quitting, or is the master giving the servant two weeks' notice before letting her go? In other words, is Dora or Freud in the role of the governess? Cixous's play gives a double reading to this, leaving the distribution of roles ambiguous. On page 98 Freud says: 'A fortnight? That's the notice a governess gives of her departure.' In this reading the departing one, Dora, is the governess. But on page 82, in response to Dora's complaint that the cure is lasting too long, Freud says: 'You still need a helper for several months.' Dora replies, 'I don't need a governess.' Perhaps the only respect in which this ambiguity can be decided is economic. Freud is being paid by Dora's family; he is the servant whose services are no longer required. I certainly do not wish to deny the Dora–governess identification, but merely to emphasize what is *not* analyzed in Freud's text.

As Cixous points out (*La jeune née*, p. 276), there are two governesses in Dora's story and both suffer the same fate–seduced and abandoned by the master. When Freud makes the governess connection in Dora's last session, she recalls the K's governess, who had been seduced by Herr K with the same words he then tries to use on Dora. When Dora transfers her relation to Herr K onto Freud, she refuses to be dismissed as the governess was. Her revenge is to switch roles and put Herr K/Freud into the place of the servant and dismiss him.

The identification between Freud and the governess does not merely result from Dora's revenge reversal. Dora told how *her* governess appeared to be interested in Dora until Dora realized the governess was really just interested in Dora's father (Freud, p. 37). Octave Mannoni, in his *Fictions freudiennes* (1978), has Dora write a letter to Frau K in which she says that Freud, likewise, 'was not really interested in me, but only in pleasing papa' (p. 15). If it is the case that Freud is using Dora to get to her father–that, as Mannoni has Dora say, Freud is 'in love with papa' (ibid.)–then it is ironic that Freud should suffer the same fate as the governess, to be rejected by Dora's father. Freud writes at the end of the case-history that '*it must be confessed* that Dora's father was *never entirely straightforward*. He had *given his support* to the treatment so long as he could hope that I should "talk" Dora out of her belief that there was something more than a friendship between him and Frau K. *His interest faded* when he observed that it was not my intention to bring about that result' (p. 109, my italics). 'It must be confessed' suggests that there is some shame attached to this for Freud. He has been taken in, believing in this man's 'interest' and 'support', and then discovering he was merely being used.

Identification between Freud and a governess, maid or nurse is not restricted to the confines of the Dora case, but has a decisive, structural relation to psychoanalysis in general. Psychoanalysis–Freud was discovering at the time of the Dora case but not 'in time'–works because of the transference, because the patient transfers previous relations with others onto the psychoanalyst, reactivates the emotions, and can work them out in analysis.

Later Freud will theorize that all relations to others merely repeat the child's original relation to the mother, the first other. Transference is not peculiar to psychoanalysis, but is actually the structure of all love. Even the relation to the father, Freud discovered, is already actually a transference of mother-love onto the father. What distinguishes psychoanalysis from other relations is the possibility of analyzing the transference, of being aware of the emotions as a repetition, as inappropriate to context. Whereas in other relationships, both parties have an investment in seeing love not as a repetition but as unique and particular to the person loved, in psychoanalysis the analyst will want to point out the structure of repetition. What facilitates the recognition of the feeling as transference, as an inappropriate repetition, is the fact that the analyst is paid. The money proves that the analyst is only a stand-in. Rather than having the power of life and death like the mother has over the infant, the analyst is financially dependent on the patient. But, in that case, the original 'analyst', the earliest person paid to replace the mother is that frequent character is Freud's histories, the nursemaid/governess.

And she is, as both Clément and Cixous agree (*La jeune née*, p. 276), the ultimate seductress. Just as the Dora case poses for Freud the 'riddle' of the source of Dora's sexual knowledge, hysteria in general poses the enigma of a seduction, that is, likewise, an initiation into carnal knowledge. In the first section of *La jeune née* ('La Coupable'–The Guilty Woman), Clément traces Freud's search for the guilty one, search for the seducer. Freud begins with the discovery that hysterics were seduced by their fathers. But, unable to accept the possibility of so many perverse fathers, he presses on to the discovery of infantile, polymorphous perverse, sexuality. Not fathers but children are perverse: they fantasize seduction by the father. But his detective work does not stop there. Perhaps because he is a father and was a child, he goes on to locate the guilt where it will not besmirch him. Escaping Oedipus's fate, Freud's search for the original sin will end up exculpating him as father/child. In the 1933 lecture 'Femininity' he writes, 'And now we find the phantasy of seduction once more in the pre-Oedipus. . . but the seducer is regularly the mother. Here, however, the phantasy touches the ground of reality, for it was really the mother who by her activities over the child's bodily hygiene inevitably stimulated, and perhaps even roused for the first time, pleasurable sensations in her genitals'.[5]

Whereas the fantasy of the father's seduction is mere fantasy, the mother's seduction 'touches the ground of reality'. This 'ground of reality', the mother's actual role in child-raising assures that there is no realistic ground for identification between Freud and the mother. The riddle is solved; the mother is 'the source' of sexuality, of perversion, of neurosis. The detective work is completed.

Or it would be completed if the family were truly a closed circuit. One of psychoanalysis's consistent errors is to reduce everything to a family paradigm. Sociopolitical questions are always brought back to the model father–mother–child. Class conflict and revolution are understood as a repetition of parent–child relations. This has always been the pernicious apoliticism of psychoanalysis. It has also been hard to argue against without totally rejecting psychoanalysis, since it is based upon the fundamental notion that everything we do as adults must repeat some infantile wish, and for most of us, the infantile world was the family. What is necessary to get beyond this dilemma is a recognition that the closed, cellular model of the family used in such psychoanalytic thinking is an idealization, a secondary revision of the family. The family never was, in any of Freud's texts, completely closed off from questions of economic class. And the most insistent locus of that intrusion into the family circle (intrusion of the symbolic into the imaginary) is the maid/governess/nurse. As Cixous says, 'she is the hole in the social cell' (*La jeune née*, p. 276)[6].

The search for the seducer is not complete when it has interrogated all the family members: father–child–mother. 'Femininity', the text just quoted in which Freud declares the mother's seduction as grounded in reality, might be considered a secondary revision of an earlier text, 'Female Sexuality'. In this earlier text we read: 'The part played in starting [phallic activity] by nursery hygiene is reflected in the very common phantasy which makes the mother or nurse into a seducer.... Actual seduction, too, is common enough; it is initiated either by other children or someone in charge of the child [nursemaid] who wants to soothe it, or send it to sleep or make it dependent on them.'[7]

It has become a commonplace of the history of psychoanalysis to mark as a turning-point the moment in the 1890s when Freud stopped believing in a 'real' seduction at the origin of hysteria and realized that the source of neurosis is the child's fantasies. This is the monumental break with theories of traumatic etiology and the discovery of infantile sexuality. But here in a 1931 text, Freud is talking about 'actual seduction'. The father cannot be a seducer, that would undercut his upright position as patriarch. Even the mother only seduces unwittingly in the execution of her proper duties. The 'actual seduction', intentional seduction, can only be the act of another child (children not parents are perverse) or a nurse. The servant, member of a lower class, like a child, is capable of perversion.

The discovery of the universal fantasy of seduction by the father is Freud's discovery of the Oedipus complex. From that, via *Totem and Taboo*, we reach an incest taboo which formulated by Lévi-Strauss will found society by keeping sexual relations outside the family circle. If sexual relations are understood as some kind of contact with alterity (although generally there is some ritual homogenization of that alterity), then the incest taboo would institute a prohibition against alterity within the family circle, a law ensuring the 'imaginary' closure of the cell. In that case, the 'nurse'–not only outside the family, but outside the economic class–would constitute the greatest threat to the law homogenizing the family. Lévi-Strauss finds that the correlate to the incest taboo is endogamy. Sexual relations are with someone whose alterity is limited within the confines of a larger circle. Exogamy, marrying outside the larger circle, is equally a violation of the incest taboo. Marriage outside of class or race might represent a contact with a non-assimilable alterity, thus like actual incest bringing unmitigated heterogeneity within the family circle. Freud's nurses and governesses might represent just such otherness, the very otherness that can also be represented by the violence of class conflict. Yet she is there at the heart of the family, in the cell nucleus. She is so much a part of the family that the child's fantasies (the unconscious) do not distinguish 'mother or nurse'.

The question Clément asked about the hysteric must be asked about the governess. Does she contest or conserve? Is she a heroine or a victim? Is she a hole in the cell (as Cixous says), or does the cell close up around her again? 'Open' or 'shut' cannot be a matter of indifference. Of course the answer is that her role is ambiguous. ('I was "sure" you would say that.') The determining question is one of symbolic inscription. The apolitical psychoanalytic thinking that has traditionally reduced economic questions to 'family matters' is simply an avatar of familial thinking. The familial imaginary wants to preserve the infantile fantasmatic confusion between mother and nurse. If the nurse is assimilated to the mother (if the transference goes unquestioned) then the family cell can close up again.

Psychoanalysis can be and ought to be the place of symbolic inscription of the governess. The absolute importance of the economic transaction between patient and analyst has been repeatedly stressed by analytic theory. Despite this, there is a strong temptation to be the Mother (the phallic mother, Lacan's Other, the subject presumed to know, the Doctor) rather than the nurse. Freud, for example, used to raise money to support the Wolf-Man, after the latter was impoverished. The Wolf-Man is the classic case of a patient who never resolved the transference, who remained 'Freud's Wolf-Man' for the rest of his life. How can the transference be analyzed if the economic rupture of the imaginary is sutured, if the financial distinction between governess and mother effaced? For psychoanalysis to be a locus of radical contestation, Freud must assume his identification with the governess.

Cixous says in *La jeune née*, 'the truth is that, in the system of exchange, me in your place and you in my place...Freud in relation to Dora occupied the maid's place. It is Freud who was the maid, and that is what is intolerable for Freud in the Dora case, it's to have been treated like maids were treated: to have been thrown out like maids were thrown out' (p. 280). The vulgar, idiomatic expression Cixous uses for 'thrown out' is 'foutu à la porte'. 'Foutre', which no longer has a literal sense, used to mean 'fuck'. What Freud could not tolerate was to 'have been *foutu à la porte* (fucked at the door) like maids were fucked at the door'. I take leave for this vulgar, literal reading from Cixous's emphasis on the door feature in Dora (*Porte-trait de Door-a*), which keeps the door in this commonplace idiom from fading into a figurative background. Once the door is noticed, 'foutre' is unavoidable. The maid is 'fucked at the door'. She is 'at the door' inasmuch as she is a threshold figure: existing between 'within the family' and 'outside the family'. Fucking her is a threshold act, somewhere between incest and exogamy, participating in both, embracing the outside all the while attempting to assimilate it. If 'open' or 'shut' is not a matter of indifference, as Freud would have it, then 'foutre' always takes place 'at the door'. It is not just the maid, but in Freud's 'well-known' symbolism, women in general who are 'foutues à la porte'.

As Cixous points out (*La jeune née*, p. 281), the Dora case is punctuated by women being declared 'nothing'. Both Herr K and Dora's father say that of their wives.[8] What is true of the wives (mothers) is even more explicit for the two governesses. Dora 'sees a massacre of women executed to make space for her. But she knows that she will in turn be massacred' (Cixous, *La jeune née*, p. 282). Neither Dora, the hysteric, nor Freud, the governess, can tolerate the position allotted them by the system of exchanges. Neither Dora nor Freud can tolerate identification with the seduced and abandoned governess.

As threatening representative of the symbolic, the economic, the extra-familial, the maid must be both seduced (assimilated) and abandoned (expelled). She must be 'foutue à la porte'. The nurse is desirable: her alterity is a stimulus, a tension, a disturbing itch in the composure of the family. But the desire for her is murderous. Sexual seduction (ritual homogenizing assimilation) is not sufficient to reduce the stimulus tension. Her alterity is not just her femininity, not even just her not belonging to the family, it is her not belonging to the same economic class. It is not enough to seduce her; she must be expelled from the family.

Dora and Freud cannot bear to identify with the governess because they think there is a still some place where one can escape the structural exchange of women. They still believe that there is some mother who is not a governess. Both Dora and Freud dismiss Dora's mother: she is obviously not the phallic mother. But Dora refuses to blame or resent Frau K, refuses to see the similarity between Frau K and the governess who was using Dora to please Dora's father. Her love for Frau K—the adoration of her that is brought out by Cixous's play, as well as Lacan's reading of the Dora case[9]—is a belief in her phallic uniqueness, her unsubstitutability. That she should be compared to the Madonna (by Lacan and Cixous) is instructive in this regard.

Freud's and Dora's understanding of the 'barter' of women never passes through the general term 'des femmes', always remains in the imaginary. The imaginary might be characterized as the realm of non-assumption of the mother's castration. In the imaginary, the 'mother', unlike the maid, is assumed to be still phallic; omnipotent and omniscient, she is unique. What shows in the Dora case that neither Dora nor Freud wanted to see is that

Frau K and Dora's mother are in the same position as the maid. In feminist or symbolic or economic terms the mother/wife is in a position of substitutability and economic inferiority. For the analysis to pass out of the imaginary, it must pass through a symbolic third term—like 'des femmes' on the cover of Cixous's *Portrait de Dora*, a term that represents a class.

Having reached a definite conclusion, there remains more to say. The 'more' revolves around Dora's love for Frau K, around her lesbianism. This supplementary postscript would repeat Freud's gesture of emphasizing Dora's homosexual love in a footnote to his conclusion.

What has been said of that love in the present text is that Dora sees Frau K as the phallic mother, infallible, non-substitutable. My argument has subordinated this homosexual love to the important psychoanalytic and feminist question of the relation between transference and radical contestation. Dora's love for Frau K has been cited here as an instance of the imaginary, which is to be taken as a criticism. But the 'more' I have to say is about the beauty, the eroticism, the affirmative quality of that love, a side brought out particularly by Cixous's *Portrait*. And somehow beauty and affirmation, sexuality as pleasure and joy rather than as murderous assimilation, seem to find their place only as a supplement to the political, theoretical argument.

This afterthought also repeats a gesture Cixous makes in the dialogue at the end of *La jeune née*. She says that Dora 'saw the ignominy and the staging of the murder of woman. *One should add to that* what there is in Dora of a very beautiful, staggering, feminine homosexuality, what there is of love of woman' (p. 282, my italics). The first sentence quoted here is the climax of Cixous's argument that Dora saw and refused the 'massacre' involved in the 'barter' of woman. This is the political analysis which constitutes Cixous's reading of the Dora case. But rather than conclude there, Cixous feels the need of something more, so she continues mid-paragraph: 'One should add to that'. Perhaps in a theoretical text one can never do more than say 'there is more, there is love and beauty' which is a necessary affirmative supplement to the murderous negation that theory must be. But in *Portrait de Dora*, in the theatrical text, in the fiction, this is not a problem, the affirmative is interwoven in various patterns with the negative.[10].

The argument I conclude above, before this postscript, accepts Clément's valuation of symbolic inscription. The symbolic is politically healthy; the imaginary is regressive. That is a classic Lacanian ethical hierarchy. But like all hierarchies, it can be oppressive. One of the effects of this hierarchy, of all hierarchies (Cixous suggests, *La jeune née*, pp. 115–17), is to support the valuation of men over women. The symbolic is linked to the Law of the Father, to the Phallus; whereas the imaginary is linked to the relation to the Mother. There have been some thinkers who have questioned this valuation of the symbolic at the expense of the imaginary. Two of the most eloquent in their questioning are Jean Laplanche and Michèle Montrelay.[11] Both argue that Lacanian analysts have been so preoccupied with denouncing the ego and thus the imaginary (for the ego is the agency of the imaginary), that they have overlooked the positive and necessary function of the imaginary. Lacanian theory views the imaginary as a 'pure effect of the symbolic', but it might also be said that the imaginary is necessary to give 'consistency' to the symbolic (Montrelay), to 'embody' it (Laplanche). Since the imaginary embodies, fleshes out the skeletal symbolic, it is possible to see the Lacanian devaluation of the imaginary as related to a hatred of the flesh, of woman and of pleasure.

Clément denies her love for the hysterics–'I really liked them, but they no longer exist'–whereas she accuses Cixous of really liking Dora. Clément has passed into the symbolic and wants to keep this love safely behind her, in the past tense, does not want to regress into the imaginary. Dora's love for Frau K is marked in Freud's text by Dora's phrase 'her adorable white body' (p. 61). In Cixous's play Dora describes this body as 'pearly' (p. 34). Yet Clément, in her section of *La jeune née,* calls Dora 'the pearl of the hysterics' (p. 96). It is not that Clément does not love Dora, but that she wants to deny that love, the beauty of the pearl, wants to be firmly ensconced in the symbolic, with no ambiguity.

It cannot be a question here of choosing Clément's symbolic or Cixous's imaginary. Indeed, the fact that the two are bound together into one book frustrates traditional notions of opposition. Like the hysteric's role, like the governess's role, we must learn to accept the ambiguity, learn to make 'open or shut' a matter of indifference. Both Clément and Cixous use the word 'bisexual' in their texts in *La jeune née* to name some sort of positive goal. Bisexuality has traditionally been linked with hysteria in psychoanalytic theory. But these women writers are talking about an 'other bisexuality'. Neither the fantasmatic resolution of differences in the imaginary, nor the fleshless, joyless assumption of the fact of one's lack of unity in the symbolic, but an other bisexuality, one that pursues, loves and accepts both the imaginary and the symbolic, both theory and flesh.

Notes and References

All translations from Lacan's *Écrits* (Éditions du Seuil, 1966) are mine unless otherwise noted. When a quotation from Lacan can also be found in Alan Sheridan's translation–*Écrits: A Selection* (Tavistock and Norton, 1977)–that page reference is also given, and the translation referred to as 'Sheridan'.

CHAPTER 1: *PSYCHOANALYSIS AND FEMINISM*

1 Juliet Mitchell, *Psychoanalysis and Feminism* (Allen Lane and Pantheon, 1974; Pelican Book, 1975; same pagination throughout these different editions).
2 'The Signification of the Phallus' in *Écrits*, p. 690. Also Sheridan, pp. 285–6.
3 'L'Instance de la lettre dans l'inconscient' in *Écrits*. The translation here used is by Jan Miel in *Structuralism*, ed. Jacques Ehrmann (Anchor Books, 1970). Also found in Sheridan as 'The Agency of the Letter in the Unconscious'.
4 *Écrits*, p. 500; Miel, op. cit., pp. 108–9; Sheridan, p. 152.
5 *Écrits*, p. 501; Miel, op. cit., p. 109; Sheridan, p. 152.
6 'The Subversion of the Subject and the Dialectic of Desire in the Freudian Unconscious', in *Écrits*, p. 804; Sheridan, p. 302.

CHAPTER 2: OF PHALLIC PROPORTIONS: LACANIAN CONCEIT

1 The reference is to the title of Freud's 1925 article 'Some Psychical Consequences of the Anatomical Distinction between the Sexes', *The Standard Edition of The Complete Psychological Works* (Hogarth Press, 1953–74) vol. XIX.
2 'La Signification du phallus' and 'Propos directifs pour un congrès sur la sexualité féminine' in *Écrits*. The former appears in Sheridan as 'The Signification of the Phallus'.
3 Ernest Jones, *Papers on Psycho-Analysis,* 5th edn (Baillière, Tindall & Cox, 1948) p. 103.

4 Jones, 'The Early Development of Female Sexuality', in *Papers on Psycho-analysis*, p. 438.

5 Jean Laplanche and Jean-Baptiste Pontalis, *The Language of Psycho-analysis*, trans. Donald Nicholson-Smith (Hogarth, 1973). There have been two English translations of *Verleugnung*–disavowal and denial. Nicholson-Smith chooses to use 'disavowal', but his long discussion of the alternative leaves the question open. I obviously prefer 'denial', in this context, for its resonance with Jones's text.

6 Some notion of disproportion seems to underly statements of Jones's such as: 'The all-important *part* normally played in male sexuality by the genital organs naturally tends to make us *equate* castration with the abolition of sexuality *altogether*. . . . With women, where the *whole penis idea* is always *partial* and mostly *secondary* in nature, this should be still more evident' (*Papers on Psycho-Analysis*, pp. 439–40, my italics).

7 See *Écrits*, p. 505; Sheridan, p. 156.

8 See for example, 'L'Instance de la lettre dans l'inconscient ou la raison depuis Freud', p. 509 (Sheridan, 'The Agency of the Letter in the Unconscious or Reason since Freud', p. 158) and 'La Chose freudienne', p. 410 (Sheridan, 'The Freudian Thing', p. 122).

9 Laplanche and Pontalis, *The Language of Psycho-analysis*, p. 412.

10 *Manque-à-être*: want-to-be, in Lacan's own English translation (see Sheridan, p. xi).

11 Freud, 'Femininity', in *New Introductory Lectures on Psycho-Analysis, Standard Edition*, vol. XXII, p. 134.

12 *Civilization and its Discontents, Standard Edition*, vol. XXI, p. 99.

13 'Recherches sur la féminité, *Critique*, 278 (July 1970) p. 655. Also found in Michèle Montrelay, *L'Ombre et le nom* (Editions de Minuit, 1977) p. 59. Translated as 'Inquiry into Femininity', *m/f*, 1 (1978). The book she is reviewing is edited by Janine Chasseguet-Smirgel (University of Michigan Press, 1970). It was originally published in French as *Recherches psychanalytiques sur la sexualité féminine* (Payot, 1964). Montrelay's choice of the Italian phrase 'odor di femina' may echo Lacan's use of that phrase in his 'Seminar on the Purloined Letter' (*Écrits*, p. 35). The English translation of that seminar by Jeffrey Mehlman can be found in *Yale French Studies*, 48 (1972) p. 66.

14 Béla Grunberger, 'Outline for a Study of Narcissism in Female Sexuality', in *Female Sexuality: New Psychoanalytic Views* ed. J. Chasseguet-Smirgel (University of Michigan Press, 1970), p. 76.

15 See *Écrits*, pp. 503–5; Sheridan, pp. 154–6.

CHAPTER 3: THE LADIES' MAN

1 Lacan, *Le Séminaire livre* xx: *Encore* (Éditions du Seuil, 1975) p. 75.
2 See Jacques Derrida, *Spurs/Éperons* (University of Chicago Press, 1979) pp. 58–61; and Derrida, 'The Purveyor of Truth', *Yale French Studies*, 52 (1975) pp. 96–7.
3 Lacan, *Le Séminaire livre* xi: *les quatre concepts fondamentaux de la psychanalyse* (Éditions du Seuil, 1972) p. 38.
4 Luce Irigaray, *Speculum de l'autre femme* ('Editions de Minuit, 1974) p. 41.
5 Lacan, *Télévision* (Éditions du Seuil, 1973).
6 See Freud, 'Fetishism', *Standard Edition* vol. xxi.

CHAPTER 4: *ENCORE* ENCORE

1 Stephen Heath, 'Difference', *Screen*, vol. 19, 4 (Winter 1978/79) pp. 50–112. All quotations from Heath are from this article, except where otherwise noted.
2 Lacan, *Le Séminaire livre* xx: *Encore* p. 75. All quotations from Lacan in this chapter are from this book.
3 Heath, 'Notes on Suture', *Screen*, vol. 18, 4 (Winter 1977/78).
4 Jacques-Alain Miller, 'Suture', *Screen*, vol. 18, 4 (Winter 1977/78).
5 Sigmund Freud, 'An Outline of Psycho-Analysis', *Standard Edition* vol. xxiii, p. 188.

CHAPTER 5: THE FATHER'S SEDUCTION

1 Sigmund Freud, *New Introductory Lectures on Psycho-Analysis, Standard Edition* vol. xxii, pp. 10–11. Hereafter referred to as *NIL*.
2 Shoshana Felman, 'To Open the Question', *Literature and Psychoanalysis: The Question of Reading: Otherwise, Yale French Studies*, 55–6 (1977) p. 10. All italics Felman's except 'blind spot'.
3 Luce Irigaray, *Ce Sexe qui n'en est pas un* (Editions de Minuit, 1977). In this context of questions it is interesting to notice Felman's titles: 'The Question of Reading', 'To Open the Question'.
4 *The Poems of Heine, Complete*, trans. Edgar Alfred Bowring (G. Bell and Sons, 1916) p. 260.
5 Is then the ironic lesson of Jacques Lacan's 'Seminars', which are enormous lectures, in which he functions as the only and ultimate 'subject presumed to know', that a seminar is always merely a

disguised lecture, that one does not know how to overthrow the pedagogic relation?

6 Freud, 'The Infantile Genital Organization' *Standard Edition*, vol. XIX, p. 142.

7 The most glaring of these symptomatic attempts to disengage the anal definitions from the genital can be found in a 1915 footnote to the third of Freud's *Three Essays on the Theory of Sexuality*; a footnote to Chapter 4 of *Civilization and its Discontents* (1930); and here in 'Femininity' (1933).

8 *Nouvelles Conférences sur la psychanalyse* (Gallimard, Collection Idées). This is the edition Irigaray uses.

9 The first quotation is from *Jokes and their Relation to the Unconscious*, the second from 'Constructions in Analysis'. The italics in both are mine.

10 Freud provides the model for metaphorization of faeces in 'On Transformations of Instinct as Exemplified in Anal Erotism' (1917), *Standard Edition* vol. XVII.

11 The term is Freud's from his article on '"Wild" Psychoanalysis,' *Standard Edition*, vol. XI.

12 J. Laplanche and J. B. Pontalis, *The Language of Psycho-analysis*, p. 201.

CHAPTER 6: IMPERTINENT QUESTIONS

1 Irigaray changes the title from 'All women (*tutte*) are like that' –Mozart's title–to 'All men (*tutti*) are like that'. According to Irigaray Lacan's victory is the triumph of all men.

2 Irigaray makes oblique reference to this Lacan text in her reading of Kant ('Un a priori paradoxal', *Speculum*). She writes 'Shall we place Kant with Sade here?' (Mettrons-nous là Kant avec Sade?)

3 Marquis de Sade, *La Philosophie dans le boudoir. Oeuvres complètes* (Éditions Pauvert, 1970) vol. XXV, p. 81.

4 Pierre Klossowski, *Sade mon prochain* (Éditions du Seuil, 1947).

5 A name likely to highlight a play of religious irony.

CHAPTER 7: WRITING ERRATIC DESIRE

1 See Freud on the narcissism of small differences in *Group Psychology and the Analysis of the Ego*, *Standard Edition* vol. XVIII.

2 For a discussion of representation as a way of binding anxiety, see Michèle Montrelay, 'Recherches sur la féminité'. For the deadliness of representation, see Lacan, 'Le Stade du miroir', *Écrits*, also in

Sheridan.

3 For example, see 'La Chose Freudienne', *Écrits*, also in Sheridan.

4 For further discussion of this problematic of the institutionalization of psychoanalysis see Sherry Turkle, *Psychoanalytic Politics* (Basic Books, 1978) and Francois Roustang, *Un Destin si funeste* (Éditions de Minuit, 1976).

5 See 'Le Séminaire sur "la lettre volée"', *Écrits*. Trans. by Jeffrey Mehlman in *Yale French Studies*, 48 (1972).

6 *Écrits*, p. 709.

7 *Écrits*, p. 692; Sheridan, p. 288.

8 Luce Irigaray, *Ce Sexe qui n'en est pas un* (Éditions de Minuit, 1977), p. 144, her italics.

9 I am indebted to Jacques Derrida for the phrase 'the scene of writing'. See 'Freud et la scène de l'écriture', *L'Écriture et la différence* (Éditions du Seuil, 1966), trans. by Jeffrey Mehlman in *Yale French Studies*, 48 (1972). In general, my emphasis on 'writing' in this chapter owes much to the work of Derrida.

10 Dictionary used: *Le Petit Robert* (Société du nouveau Littré, 1970).

11 Charles T. Lewis and Charles Short, *A Latin Dictionary* (Oxford University Press, 1966).

12 Montrelay, *L'Ombre et le nom*, p. 139n.

13 Cf. Lacan's play with the 'bar' and the minus sign, *Écrits*, p. 515; *Écrits: A Selection*, p. 164.

CHAPTER 8: THE PHALLIC MOTHER: FRAUDIAN ANALYSIS

1 For excellent work on this structurally weak distinction being done by American psychoanalytic feminists see Nancy Chodorow, *The Reproduction of Mothering* (University of California Press, 1978) and Dorothy Dinnerstein, *The Mermaid and the Minotaur* (Harper & Row, 1976).

2 Julia Kristeva, *Des Chinoises* (Éditions des femmes, 1974) p. 35. Trans. as *About Chinese Women* (Urizen Press, 1979). The quotations here are, nonetheless, my translations.

3 Kristeva, 'L'Héréthique de l'amour', *Tel Quel*, 74 (Winter 1977) p. 35.

4 See 'L'Héréthique', pp. 45–6.

5 Kristeva, *Polylogue* (Éditions du Seuil, 1977) p. 409.

6 'The Signification of the Phallus', *Écrits*, p. 692; Sheridan, p. 288.

7 'The Freudian Thing', *Écrits*, p. 409; Sheridan, p. 121.

8 For a discussion of this anxiety, see Michèle Montrelay, 'Inquiry into Femininity', *m/f*, 1 (1978).

9 Note that *Des Chinoises* is published by Éditions des femmes, which is run by a group of women called 'Psychoanalysis and Politics'.

10 Kristeva, 'L'Autre du sexe', *Sorcières*, 10, pp. 37–40.

CHAPTER 9: KEYS TO DORA

1 Catherine Clément/Hélène Cixous, *La jeune née* (Union Générale d' Éditions, Collection '10/18', 1975) p. 184.

2 Sigmund Freud, 'Fragment of an Analysis of a Case of Hysteria', *Standard Edition* vol. VII, p. 67 n.

3 There is one other example in the Dora case where the English translation uses a French phrase to render Freud's German: 'And if the connection between the symptomatic expression and the unconscious mental content should strike us as being in this case a clever *tour de force*, we shall be glad to hear it succeeds in creating the same impression in every other case and in every other instance.' Again what Freud is discussing here is the scandalous discovery that the unconscious speaks. The French work which insists on his discovery might be suspected by Anglophones as a 'clever *tour de force*', that is artful and far-fetched rather than serious and scientific.

4 In the next paragraph Freud uses another French expression–'pour faire une omelette il faut casser des oeufs' (you have to break eggs to make an omelette)–still in the context of his defence of sexual conversation with his hysterics. Yet even this culinary commonplace can take on a sexual meaning. Lacan, in 'Position de l'inconscient' (*Écrits*), rewrites 'omelette' into its near homonym 'hommelette'–homunculus or little man. One could, following that lead, read the proverb as meaning 'you have to break eggs [penetrate and fertilize ova] to make a little man [a baby]'.

5 Freud, *New Introductory Lectures*, *Standard Edition,* vol. XXII, p. 120.

6 *La jeune née*, p. 276. There is a nurse in Freud's own infancy who plays an important role and is connected to 'cases' and being 'locked up'. She was expelled from the house and locked up for theft. See Ernest Jones, *Sigmund Freud: Life and Work*, (Basic Books, 1953) vol. I. For some excellent work on the import of Freud's nurse, see Jim Swan, '*Mater* and Nannie', *American Imago*, vol. 31, 1 (Spring 1974).

7 Freud, 'Female Sexuality', *Standard Edition*, vol. XXI, p. 232.

8 Actually in the English translation they say 'I get nothing out of my wife', whereas Cixous has them say in French 'My wife is nothing for me'. Probably the most literal translation of the German–'Ich habe

nichts an meiner Frau'–would be 'I have nothing in my wife'. What seems to work, regardless of the language, is an insistent association between wife and 'nothing'.

9 See Lacan's excellent and unusually clear 'Intervention sur le transfert', *Écrits*.

10 But must we accept this inevitable division? Cannot a theoretical text also be theatrical? 'Theatre' and 'theory' both stem from the same root–'thea'. In fact, is theory not always theatrical, a rhetorical performance as well as a quest for truth? The limits of theory remain to be tested.

11 Michèle Montrelay, *L'Ombre et le nom*, pp. 155–6. Laplanche, *Life and Death in Psychoanalysis*, trans. Jeffrey Mehlman (Johns Hopkins University Press, 1976) pp. 125–6.

Bibliography

Chasseguet-Smirgel, Janine (ed.), *Female Sexuality: New Psychoanalytic Views* (University of Michigan Press, 1970).

Chodorow, Nancy, *The Reproduction of Mothering* (University of California Press, 1978).

Cixous, Hélène, *Portrait de Dora* (Éditions des femmes, 1976).

Clément, Catherine, 'Un numéro', *L'Arc*, 58 (1974).

_____ and Hélène Cixous, *La jeune née* (Union Générale d'Éditions, Collection '10/18', 1975).

Derrida, Jacques, 'Freud and the Scene of Writing', trans. Jeffrey Mehlman, *Yale French Studies*, 48 (1972).

_____, 'The Purveyor of Truth', trans. W. Domingo, J. Hulbert, M. Ron and M.-R. Logan, *Yale French Studies*, 52 (1975).

_____, *Spurs/Éperons* (University of Chicago Press, 1979).

Dinnerstein, Dorothy, *The Mermaid and the Minotaur* (Harper & Row, 1976).

Felman, Shoshana 'La Méprise et sa chance', *L'Arc*, 58 (1974).

_____, 'To Open the Question', *Yale French Studies*, 55-6 (1978/79).

Freud, Sigmund *Civilization and its Discontents, The Standard Edition of the Complete Psychological Works* (Hogarth Press, 1953-74) vol. XXI.

_____, 'Constructions in Analysis', *Standard Edition,* vol. XXIII.

_____, 'Female Sexuality', *Standard Edition,* vol. XXI.

_____, 'Fetishism', *Standard Edition,* vol. XXI.

_____, 'Fragment of an Analysis of a Case of Hysteria', *Standard Edition,* vol. VII.

_____, *Group Psychology and the Analysis of the Ego, Standard Edition,* vol. XVIII.

_____, 'The Infantile Gential Organization', *Standard Edition,* vol. XIX.

_____, *Jokes and Their Relation to the Unconscious, Standard Edition,* vol. VIII.

_____, *New Introductory Lectures on Psycho-Analysis, Standard Edition,* vol. XXII.

_____, *Nouvelles Conférences sur la psychanalyse* (Gallimard, Collection Idées).

_____, '"Wild" Psychoanalysis', *Standard Edition,* vol. XI.

_____, 'On Transformations of Instinct as Exemplified in Anal Erotism', *Standard Edition*, vol. XVII.

_____, 'Some Psychical Consequences of the Anatomical Distinction between the Sexes', *Standard Edition*, vol. XIX.

_____, *Totem and Taboo, Standard Edition*, vol. XIII.

Grunberger, Béla 'Outline for a Study of Narcissism in Female Sexuality', *Female Sexuality: New Psychoanalytic Views* (see Chasseguet-Smirgel (ed.)).

Heath, Stephen 'Difference', *Screen*, vol. 19, 4 (Winter 1978/79).

_____, 'Notes on Suture', *Screen*, vol. 18, 4 (Winter 1977/78).

Heine, Heinrich *The Poems, Complete*, trans. Edgar Alfred Bowring (G. Bell and Sons, 1916).

Irigaray, Luce *Ce Sexe qui n'en est pas un* (Éditions de Minuit, 1977).

_____, *Et l'une ne bouge pas sans l'autre* (Éditions de Minuit, 1979).

_____, 'La "Mécanique" des fluides', *L'Arc*, 58 (1974).

_____, 'La Misère de la psychanalyse', *Critique*, 365 (October 1977).

_____, *Speculum de l'autre femme* (Éditions de Minuit, 1974).

Jones, Ernest 'The Early Development of Female Sexuality', *Papers on Psycho-Analysis*, 5th edn (Baillière, Tindal & Cox, 1948).

_____, 'Early Female Sexuality', *Papers on Psycho-Analysis*.

_____, *Sigmund Freud: Life and Work* (Basic Books, 1953) vol. 1.

_____, 'The Theory of Symbolism', *Papers on Psycho-Analysis*.

Kristeva, Julia *About Chinese Women* (Urizen Press, 1979).

_____, 'L'Autre du sexe', *Sorcières*, 10.

_____, *Des Chinoises* (Éditions des femmes, 1974).

_____, 'L'Héréthique de l'amour', *Tel Quel*, 74 (Winter 1977).

_____, 'Un nouveau type d'intellectuel: le dissident'. *Tel Quel*, 74 (Winter 1977).

_____, *Polylogue* (Éditions du Seuil, 1977).

Lacan, Jacques 'A la mémoire d'Ernest Jones: Sur sa théorie du symbolisme', *Écrits* (Éditions du Seuil, 1966).

_____, 'The Agency of the Letter in the Unconscious', *Écrits: A Selection*, trans. Alan Sheridan (Tavistock and Norton, 1977).

_____, 'La Chose freudienne', *Écrits*.

_____, 'The Freudian Thing', *Écrits: A Selection*.

_____, *The Four Fundamental Concepts of Psycho-Analysis*, trans. Alan Sheridan (Hogarth and Norton, 1976).

_____, 'The Insistence of the Letter in the Unconscious', trans. Jan Miel, *Structuralism* (Anchor Books, 1970).

_____, 'L'Instance de la lettre dans l'inconscient', *Écrits*.

_____, 'Intervention sur le transfert', *Écrits*.

_____, 'Kant avec Sade', *Écrits*.

_____, 'The Mirror Stage', *Écrits: A Selection*.

_____, 'Position de l'inconscient', *Écrits*.

_____, 'Propos directifs pour un congrès sur la sexualité féminine', *Écrits*.

_____, *Le Séminaire livre XI: les quatre concepts fondamentaux de la psychanalyse* (Éditions du Seuil, 1973).

_____, *Le Séminaire livre XX: Encore* (Éditions du Seuil, 1975).

_____, 'Séminaire sur "La Lettre volée"', *Écrits*.

_____, 'Seminar on the Purloined Letter', trans. Jeffrey Mehlman, *Yale French Studies*, 48 (1972).

_____, 'La Signification du phallus', *Écrits*.

_____, 'The Signification of the Phallus', *Écrits: A Selection*.

_____, 'Le Stade du miroir', *Écrits*.

_____, 'La Subversion du sujet et la dialectique du désir', *Écrits*.

_____, 'The Subversion of the Subject and the Dialectic of Desire', *Ecrits: A Selection*.

_____, *Télévision* (Éditions du Seuil, 1973).

Laplanche, Jean *Life and Death in Psychoanalysis*, trans. Jeffrey Mehlman (Johns Hopkins University Press, 1976).

_____, and Pontalis, Jean-Baptiste, *The Language of Psycho-Analysis*, trans. Donald Nicholson-Smith (Hogarth Press, 1973).

Leclaire, Serge *On tue un enfant* (Éditions du Seuil, 1975).

Lemoine-Luccioni, Eugénie *Partage des femmes* (Éditions du Seuil, 1976).

Luccioni, Eugénie review of *Speculum*, *Esprit*, 444 (March 1975).

Mannoni, Octave, *Fictions freudiennes* (Éditions du Seuil, 1978).

Mitchell, Juliet *Psychoanalysis and Feminism* (Allen Lane and Pantheon Books, 1974).

Montrelay, Michèle 'Inquiry into Femininity', *m/f*, 1 (1978).

_____, *L'Ombre et le nom* ('Editions de Minuit, 1977).

Rousseau-Dujardin, Jacqueline 'Du temps qu'entends-je?', *L'Arc*, 58 (1974).

Roustang, Francois *Un Destin si funeste* (Éditions de Minuit, 1976).

Sade, D. A. F., Marquis de *La Philosophie dans le boudoir. Oeuvres complètes*, vol. xxv (Éditions Pauvert, 1970).

Swan, Jim '*Mater* and Nannie', *American Imago*, vol. 31, 1 (Spring 1974).

Turkle, Sherry *Psychoanalytic Politics* (Basic Books, 1978).

Index